P9-DMO-947

ECONOMICS EXPLAINED

EVERYTHING YOU NEED TO KNOW ABOUT
HOW THE ECONOMY WORKS AND WHERE IT'S
GOING

*Robert Heilbroner
and Lester Thurow*

NEWLY REVISED AND UPDATED

A TOUCHSTONE BOOK
Published by Simon & Schuster

TOUCHSTONE
Rockefeller Center
1230 Avenue of the Americas
New York, NY 10020

Copyright © 1982, 1987, 1994, 1998 by Robert Heilbroner and Lester Thurow

All rights reserved,
including the right of reproduction
in whole or in part in any form.

First Touchstone Edition 1982

The boxed material in this book and the Appendix on banking are taken directly
from Robert Heilbroner and Lester Thurow, *The Economic Problem,* 6th ed.,
Prentice-Hall, 1980

TOUCHSTONE and colophon are registered trademarks
of Simon & Schuster Inc.
Manufactured in the United States of America

10   9   8   7   6   5   4   3   2   1

Library of Congress Cataloging-in-Publication Data

Heilbroner, Robert L.
    Economics explained : everything you need to know about how the
economy works and where it's going / Robert L. Heilbroner and Lester C.
Thurow. — Newly rev. and updated.
        p.   cm.
    Originally published: Englewood Cliffs, N.J.. : Prentice-Hall. 1982.
    Includes index.
    1. Economics.   2. United States—Economic conditions—1945–
I. Thurow, Lester C.   II. Title.
HB171.H479   1998
330—dc21   98-11544
                                                         CIP

ISBN 0-684-84641-1

Contents

III Microeconomics—The Anatomy of the Market System

IV Problems

Introduction

Just in case the reader-to-be hasn't noticed, disturbing things are going on in the American economy these days. We don't mean that American capitalism is about to give up the ghost. We do mean that changes are altering the world around us, and almost certainly will alter it further, not entirely in ways that are to our liking.

What sorts of changes? One of them is the size of that "world"—that is, the number of countries whose economic activities are closely entangled with our own. Just as an example, the computer hardware you buy in a neighborhood store was pretty much an all-American product only a few years ago. Today it is as likely to come from Korea, Taiwan, Singapore, and elsewhere, as from the U.S.A. This process is part of what is called "globalization." If it continues to grow over the next decade as rapidly as it has over the last, it could deeply affect American economic life, partly for the better—Korean video monitors cost less than American—and partly for the worse—fewer jobs in Seattle, more in Seoul.

Another change concerns income distribution. To put it bluntly, the stream of incomes going to the richest families has been growing rapidly, while the stream going to the less than affluent has been falling. Our long-term prosperity has depended to no small degree on a distribution of incomes that bolsters the buying power of working- and middle-class families. The prospect of the rich getting richer and the middle getting poorer is not one that inspires confidence in the future. Why is this happening? What can be done about it?

Yet a third upsetting tendency concerns the technology we use. We don't just mean new ways of making old things or new ways of making new things—that often "disturbing" process of invention and modernization has always been vital for capitalism. We mean that the new technologies may differ from previous ones in eliminating certain kinds of work—sometimes skilled work—without setting up a new industrial front comparable to the great technological innovations of the past. The next time you get money from an automatic teller machine (ATM) look for the ghost of the human teller whose services aren't needed any more. On those now rarer occasions when you go into a bank, ask how come there are so many fewer people behind desks than before: Could the computers on every desk have something to do with that? And when the telephone operator says "If you are calling from a touch-tone phone, press one now," ask yourself who that "operator" is.

These kinds of disturbing trends explain what is different about this edition of *Economics Explained.* There is little that is new in our explanations of how the market works or what macroeconomics means. Here, as before, we try to simplify and clarify the vocabularies and concepts you will need to understand what is going on in the economic world and whether it is working smoothly or not. But the importance accorded to the kinds of disquieting problems mentioned here is new and different. This is not only because the problems themselves are of much greater importance today than only a few years ago. Our new emphasis reflects what we believe to be the aspects of economics that our readers most want explained today.

That brings us to two last points. First, despite its focus on new and not entirely well understood problems, *Economics Explained* is not meant to be a discouraging book. On the contrary, our premise is that the period ahead could be a time of potential reward as well as heightened risk; of feasible success as well as imaginable setbacks. We want our readers to be forewarned, which is to say, forearmed.

Our second point affects the values that inform our text, as well as its analysis. There are certainly controversial opinions in this book, but they are always labeled as such, never slipped across as the Truth. As we have said in earlier editions, this is a book of teaching, not preaching. The last thing in the world we want is to persuade our readers that we know the answers to the challenges around us. But we will be very disappointed if *Economics Explained* fails to make its readers think about these challenges in ways that had not occurred to them before.

I

THE ECONOMIC BACKGROUND

ONE

Capitalism: Where Do We Come From?

We live in a capitalist economic system. Politicians constantly talk about capitalism, or if they don't like the word, about the free-enterprise system. We are constantly being told that capitalism is the wave of the future, or would be the wave of the future if only it were left alone, or sometimes that capitalism is in decline and will fall on its own weight, like the Roman Empire.

Perhaps there is no more important economic question than the future of capitalism, none that affects more deeply our private destinies and those of our children. As we will see in our next chapter, the great economists of the past were vitally concerned with this issue. Modern economists are wiser or blinder, depending on how you look at it, and say relatively little about our long-term prospects. Nonetheless, we feel that it is impossible to understand capitalism without at least some understanding of its roots. So we are going to begin the study of our economic system rather the way a doctor begins to become acquainted with a patient—by taking its history.

Many people speak about capitalism as if it were as old as the hills, as ancient as the Bible, implying that there is something about the system that accords with human nature. Yet, on reflection, this is clearly not the case. Nobody ever called the Egyptian pharaohs capitalists. The Greeks about whom Homer wrote did not comprise a business society, even though there were merchants and traders in Greece.

Medieval Europe was certainly not capitalist. Nor would anyone have used the word to describe the brilliant civilizations of India and China about which Marco Polo wrote, or the great empires of ancient Africa, or the Islamic societies of which we catch glimpses in *The Arabian Nights*.

What made these societies noncapitalist was not anything they possessed in common, for they were as different as civilizations could be, but rather, some things they *lacked* in common. To become aware of these lacks will give us a sharp sense of the uniqueness and special characteristics of capitalism itself.

To begin with, all these noncapitalist societies lacked the institution of private property. Of course, all of them recognized the right of some individuals to own wealth, often vast wealth. But none of them legally accorded the right of ownership to all persons. Land, for instance, was rarely owned by the peasants who worked it. Slaves, who were a common feature of most precapitalist systems, were only rarely permitted to own property—indeed, they *were* property. The idea that a person's property was inviolate was as unacknowledged as that his person was inviolate. The Tudor monarchs, for example, relatively enlightened as sixteenth-century monarchies went, could and did strip many a person or religious order of their possessions.

Second, none of these variegated societies possessed a central attribute of capitalism—a market system. To be sure, all of them had markets where spices, gold, slaves, cloth, pottery, and foodstuffs were offered for sale. But when we look over the expanses of ancient Asia, Africa, or the Egyptian and Roman empires, we can see nothing like the great web of transactions that binds our own economy together. Most production and most distribution took place by following the dictates of tradition or the orders of a lord. In general, only the small leftovers found their way to the market stalls. Even more important, there was no organized market at all to buy and sell land, or to hire labor, or to lend money. Markets were the ornaments of society, tradition and command its iron structure.

Under such conditions, the idea of economic freedom was held in little regard. When peasants were not free to move as they wished, when artisans were bound to their trades for life, when the relations of fieldworkers to their masters were that of serf to lord, who could worry about the right of contract or the right to withhold one's labor? The distinction is crucial in separating capitalism from what came before: A capitalist employee has the legal right to work or not work as he or she chooses, and whereas this right may seem to count for little under conditions of Dickensian poverty, it must be compared with the near-slavery of the serf legally bound to his lord's land and to the work his lord assigned him.

In such a setting, moneymaking itself was not much esteemed. Ambitious persons from the better walks of life sought fame and fortune in military exploits, in the service of the court, or in the hierarchies of religion. In this regard, it is interesting to reflect how twisted and grasping are the faces of merchants depicted by medieval artists, in contrast to the noble mien of soldiers and courtiers. Moneymaking was generally considered to be beneath a person of noble blood; indeed, in Christendom it was a pursuit uncomfortably close to sin. Usury—lending at interest—*was* a sin—in fact, a mortal sin.

As a consequence of all this, society's wealth was not owned by "the rich"—that is, by those whose main efforts were aimed directly at moneymaking—but rather by the powerful, who seized it in the struggle for lands and privileges. Of course, the winners in this struggle became rich, sometimes unimaginably rich, but their riches flowed from their power, not the other way around. Julius Caesar, for example, became rich only because he was appointed governor of Spain, from which he profited fabulously, as all provincial governors were supposed to do and did.

Last, and in some ways most significant, economic life was stable. It may not have seemed so to the peasants and merchants whose lives were constantly disrupted by war, famine, merciless taxation, and brigandage. But it was very stable compared to the tenor of economic life in our own time. The basic rhythms and techniques of economic existence were steady and repetitive. Men and women sowed and reaped, potters and metalworkers turned and hammered, weavers spun and wove—all using much the same kinds of equipment for decades, generations, sometimes centuries. How similar are the clothes and utensils, the materials of buildings, the means of conveyance that we see in the background of a Renaissance picture to those that we can make out on a Greek vase! How little material progress took place over a thousand years! That gives us a sense of how vast a change capitalism would bring when it finally burst upon the historic scene.

MARKET SOCIETY EMERGES

Thus we see that far from representing an eternal "human nature," capitalism comes as a volcanic disruption to time-honored routines of life. We begin to understand the immense inertia that prevented capitalism from developing in most earlier societies. From one of these societies to another, of course, different obstacles and barriers stood in the way of creating an economic way of life built on principles utterly alien to those that existed. But in all these societies, perhaps no barrier was more difficult to breach than the hold of tradition and command as the means of organizing economic life, and the need to substitute a market system in their place.

What is a market system? Essentially, it is one in which economic activities are left to men and women freely responding to the opportunities and discouragements of the marketplace, not to the established routines of tradition or the dictates of someone's command. Thus, in a market system most individuals are not only free to seek work where they wish, but must shop around for a job; by way of contrast, serfs or tradition-bound artisans were born to their employ and could only with great difficulty quit it for another. In a market system anyone is free to buy up land or to sell it: a farm can become a shopping center. By way of contrast again, land in most precapitalist societies was no more for sale than are the counties of our states.

Finally, a market in capital means that there is a regular flow of wealth into production—a flow of savings and investment—organized through banks and other financial companies, where borrowers pay interest as the reward for having the use of the wealth of the lenders. There was nothing like this before capitalism, except in the very small and disreputable capital markets personified in the despised moneylender.

The services of labor, land, and capital that are hired or fired in a market society are called the *factors of production,* and a great deal of economics is about how the market combines their essential contributions to production. Because they *are* essential, a question must be answered: How were the factors of production put to use prior to the market system? The answer comes as something of a shock, but it tells us a great deal.

There were no factors of production before capitalism. Of course, human labor, nature's gift of land and natural resources, and the artifacts of society have always existed. But labor, land, and capital were not commodities for sale. Labor was performed as part of the social duties of serfs or slaves, who were not paid for doing their work. Indeed, the serf paid fees to his lord for the use of the lord's equipment, and never expected to be remunerated when he turned over a portion of his crop as the lord's due. So, too, land was regarded as the basis for military power or civil administration, just as a county or state is regarded today—not as real estate to be bought and sold. And capital was thought of as treasure or as the necessary equipment of an artisan, not as an abstract sum of wealth with a market value. The idea of liquid, fluid capital would have been as strange in medieval life as would be the thought today of stocks and bonds as heirlooms never to be sold.

How did wageless labor, unrentable land, and private treasures become factors of production; that is, commodities to be bought and sold like so many yards of cloth or bushels of wheat? The answer is that a vast revolution undermined the world of tradition and command and brought into being the market relationships of the modern world. Beginning roughly in the sixteenth century—although with roots that can be traced much further back—a process of change, sometimes gradual, sometimes violent, broke the bonds and customs of the medieval world of Europe and ushered in the market society we know.

We can only touch on that long, tortuous, and sometimes bloody process here. In England the process bore with particular severity on the peasants who were expelled from their lands through the enclosure of common grazing lands. This enclosure took place to make private pasturage for the lord's sheep, whose wool had become a profitable commodity. As late as 1820 the Duchess of Sutherland evicted 15,000 tenants from 794,000 acres, replacing them with 131,000 sheep. The tenants, deprived of their traditional access to the fields, drifted into the towns, where they were forced to sell their services as a factor of production: labor.

In France the creation of factors of production bore painfully on landed property. When gold flowed into sixteenth-century Europe from the New World, prices began to rise and feudal lords found themselves in a vise. Like everything in medieval life, the rents and dues they received from the serfs were fixed and unchangeable. But the prices of merchandise were not fixed. Although more and more of the serfs' obligations were changed from kind (that is, so many dozen eggs or ells of cloth or days of labor) to cash, prices kept rising so fast that the feudal lords found it impossible to meet their bills.

Hence we begin to find a new economic individual, the *impoverished* aristocrat. In the year 1530, in the Gévaudan region of France, the richest manorial lord had an income of five thousand livres; but in towns, some merchants had incomes of sixty-five thousand livres. Thus the balance of power turned against the landed aristocracy, reducing many to shabby gentility. Meanwhile, the upstart merchants lost no time in acquiring lands that they soon came to regard not as ancestral estates but as potential capital.

This brief glance at economic history brings home an important point. The factors of production, without which a market society could not exist, are not eternal attributes of a natural order. They are the creations of a process of historic change, a change that divorced labor from social life, that created real estate out of ancestral land, and that made treasure into capital. Capitalism is the outcome of a revolutionary change—a change in laws, attitudes, and social relationships as deep and far-reaching as any in history.*

The revolutionary aspect of capitalism lies in the fact that an older, feudal way of life had to be dismantled before the market system could come into being. This brings us to think again about the element of economic freedom that plays such an important role in our definition of capitalism. For we can see that economic freedom did not arise just because men and women directly sought to shake off the bonds of custom and command. It was also thrust upon them, often as a very painful and unwelcome change.

For European feudalism, with all its cruelties and injustices, did provide a modicum of economic security. However mean a serf's life, at least he knew that in bad times he was guaranteed a small dole from his lord's granary. However exploited a journeyman, he knew that he could not be summarily thrown out of work under the rules of his master's guild. However squeezed a lord, he too knew that his rents and dues

---

*One of the many fascinating questions that surround the origins of capitalism is why it arose only in Europe and never in any other part of the world. One part of the reason is that the collapse of the Roman Empire left many towns without an allegiance to anyone. In time these towns, which were naturally centers of trading and artisan work, grew powerful and managed to bargain for privileges with kings and lords. Capitalism thus grew up in the interstices of the medieval system. A similar opportunity and stimulus did not present itself elsewhere. A controversial but important work on the rise of capitalism is Immanuel Wallerstein's *The Modern World System,* Academic Press, three vols., 1974, 1980, 1989. See also Fernand Braudel, *Capitalism and Civilization,* Harper and Row, three vols., 1981, 1982, 1984.

were secured by law and custom and would be coming in, weather permitting. Elsewhere, in China, India, and Japan, variants of this combination of tradition and command also provided an underpinning of security for economic life.

The eruption of the market system—better, the centuries-long earthquake that broke the hold of tradition and command in England and France and the Lowlands—destroyed that social underpinning. Thus the economic freedom of capitalism came as a two-edged sword. On the one hand, its new freedoms were precious achievements for those individuals who formerly had been deprived of the right to enter into legal contracts. For the up-and-coming bourgeois merchants, it was the passport to a new status in life. Even for some of the poorest classes, the freedom of economic contract was a chance to rise from a station in life from which, in earlier times, there had been almost no exit. But economic freedom also had a harsher side. This was the necessity to stay afloat by one's own efforts in rough waters where all were struggling to survive. Many a merchant and many, many a jobless worker simply disappeared from view.

The market system was thus the cause of unrest, insecurity, and individual suffering, just as it was also the cause of progress, opportunity, and fulfillment. In this contest between the costs and benefits of economic freedom lies a theme that is still a crucial issue for capitalism.

THE UNLEASHING OF TECHNOLOGY

The creation of a market society also paved the way for a change of profound significance in bringing about modern economic life. This was the incorporation of science and technology into the very midst of daily existence.

Technology is not, of course, a modern phenomenon. The gigantic stones that form prehistoric Stonehenge; the precision and delicacy of the monumental Egyptian pyramids; the Incan stone walls, fitted so exactly that a knife blade cannot be put between adjoining blocks; the Chinese Great Wall; and the Mayan observatories—all attest to mankind's long possession of the ability to transport and hoist staggering weights, to cut and shape hard surfaces, and to calculate complex problems. Indeed, many of these works would challenge our present-day engineering capabilities.

Nonetheless, although precapitalist technology reached great heights, it had a very restricted base. We have noted already that the basic tools of agriculture and artisan crafts remained little changed over millennia. Improvements came very slowly. So simple an invention as a horse collar shaped to prevent a straining animal from pressing against its windpipe did not appear during all the glories of Greece and triumphs of Rome. Not until the Middle Ages was there a switch from the ox to the draft horse as a plowing animal (a change that improved efficiency by an estimated 30 percent), or was the traditional two-field system of crop rotation improved by adopting a three-field system. (See box on page 19.) Thus was precapitalist technology lavished on the needs of rulers, priests, warriors. Its application to common, everyday work was virtually ignored.

There were, of course, good reasons why the technology of daily life was ignored. The primary effect of technological change in daily activity is to increase output, to enhance the productivity of the working person. But in a society still regulated by tradition and command, where production was carried on mainly by serfs and slaves and custombound artisans, there was little incentive to look for increases in output. The bulk of any increase in agricultural yields would only go to the lord in higher rents, not to the serf or the slave who produced them. Although a lord would benefit greatly from increases in agricultural output, how could a great noble be expected to know about, or to concern himself with, the dirty business of sowing and reaping? So, too, any artisan who altered the techniques of his trade would be expected, as a matter of course, to share these advances with his brethren. And how could his brethren, accustomed over the years to disposing of a certain quantity of pots or pans or cloth in the village market, expect to find buyers for more output? Would not the extra production simply go begging?

Thus productive technology in precapitalist societies slumbered because there was little incentive to search for change. Indeed, powerful social forces were ranged against technological change, which could only introduce an unsettling element into the world. A society whose whole way of life rested on the reproduction of established patterns of life could not imagine a world where the technology of production was constantly in flux, and where limits were no longer recognized in any endeavor.

These inhibiting forces were ruthlessly swept away by the currents of the emerging markets for labor, land, and capital. Serfs were up-

THE DIFFERENCE TECHNOLOGY MAKES:
THREE FIELDS VERSUS TWO

Until the Middle Ages, the prevailing system of cultivation was to plant half a lord's arable land in a winter crop, leaving the other half fallow. The second year, the two fields simply changed functions.

Under the three-field plan, the arable land was divided into thirds. One section was planted with a winter crop, one section with a summer crop, and one was left fallow. The second year, the first section was put into summer crops, the second section left fallow, and the third put into winter grains. In the third year, the first field was left fallow, the second used for winter crops, the third for spring planting.

Therefore, under the three-field system, only one third—not one half—of the arable land was fallow in any year. Suppose that the field as a whole yielded six hundred bushels of output. Under the two-field system, it would give an annual crop of three hundred bushels. Under the three-field system the annual crop would be two thirds of the area, or four hundred bushels—an increase of one third. Further, in those days it was customary to plow fallow land twice, and cultivated land only once. By cutting down the ratio of fallow to cultivated land, plowing time was reduced, and peasant productivity even more significantly improved. For more on this and other fascinating advances in precapitalist technology, see Lynn White, *Medieval Technology and Social Change* (Oxford: Claredon Press, 1962); and Joel Mokyr, *The Lever of Riches* (New York: Oxford University Press, 1990).

rooted to become workers forced to sell their labor power; aristocratic landlords were rudely shouldered aside by money-minded parvenus; guild masters and artisans watched commercial enterprises take away their accustomed livelihood. A new sense of necessity, of urgency, infused economic life. What had been a more or less dependable round of life became increasingly a scramble for existence. The feeling that one's economic interests were best served by following in the footsteps of one's forebears gave way to the knowledge that economic life was shot through with insecurity, and was at worst a race for survival in which each had to fend for himself or herself.

The growing importance of the market, with its impersonal pressures, radically altered the place of technology, especially in the small workshops and minuscule factories that were the staging areas of the capitalist revolution. Here the free-for-all brought a need to find toeholds in the struggle for a livelihood. And one toehold available to any aspiring capitalist with an inquiring mind and a knowledge of the actual processes of production was technology itself—some invention or improvement that would lower costs or change a product to give it an edge on its competitors.

Thus in the late eighteenth and early nineteenth centuries capitalism raised a crop of technology-minded entrepreneurs, a wholly new social group in economic history. For example, there was John Wilkinson, son of an iron producer, who became a driving force for technical change in his trade. Wilkinson insisted that everything be built of iron—pipes and bridges, bellows and cylinders (one of which powered the newfangled steam engine of John Watt). He even constructed a much-derided iron ship—later much admired! There was Richard Arkwright, barber by trade, who made his fortune by inventing (or perhaps by stealing) the first effective spinning machine, becoming in time a great mill owner. There were Peter Onions, an obscure foreman who originated the puddling process for making wrought iron; Benjamin Huntsman, a clockmaker who improved the method of making steel; and a score more. A few, like Sir Jethro Tull, a pioneer in the technology of agriculture, were great gentlemen, but on the whole the technological leaders in industry were men of humble origin.

THE INDUSTRIAL REVOLUTION

The new dynamism gave rise to the Industrial Revolution, the first chapter of a still unfinished period of history in which startling and continuous changes revolutionized both the techniques of production and the texture of daily life.

A few figures tell the story. Between 1701 and 1802, as the technology of spinning and weaving gradually was perfected, the use of cotton in England expanded by 6,000 percent. Between 1788 and 1839, when the process of iron manufacture passed through its first technological upheaval, the output of pig iron jumped from 68,000 to 1,347,000 tons. In France, in the thirty years after 1815, iron output quintupled, coal output grew sevenfold, and transportation tonnage mounted ten times. As for coal, England, the economic historian David Landes has written: "[I]n 1870 the capacity of Great Britain's steam engines was about 4 million horsepower, equivalent to the power that could be generated by 6 million horses or 40 million men. . . . [T]his many men would have eaten some 320 million bushels of wheat a year—more than three times the output of the entire United Kingdom."* It is no exaggeration to say that the Industrial Revolution rested on Watt's marvel of simple ingenuity, the steam engine.

But even these figures do not convey a full sense of the effect of technology on daily life. *Things* became more common—and more commonplace. As late as the seventeenth century, what we would consider the most ordinary possessions were scarce. A peasant counted his worldly wealth in terms of a few utensils, a table, perhaps one complete change of clothes. In his will, Shakespeare left Anne Hathaway his "second-best bed." Iron nails were so scarce that pioneers in America burned down their cottages to retrieve them. In the wilder parts of Scotland in Adam Smith's time, nails even served as money.

Technology brought a widening, deepening, ever-faster-flowing river of things. Shoes, coats, paper, window glass, chairs, buckles—objects of solicitous respect in precapitalist times for all but the privileged few—became everyday articles. Gradually capitalism gave rise to what we call a rising standard of living—a steady, regular, systematic increase in the number, variety, and quality of material goods enjoyed by the great bulk of society. No such process had ever occurred before.

A second change wrought by technology was a striking increase in the sheer size of society's industrial apparatus. The increase began with the enlargement of the equipment used in production—an enlargement that stemmed mostly from advances in the technology of iron and, later, steel. The typical furnace used in extracting iron ore increased from ten feet in height in the 1770s to over one hundred feet a century later; during the same period the crucibles in which steel was made grew from cauldrons hardly larger than an oversized jug to converters

*David Landes, *The Unbound Prometheus* (England: Cambridge University Press, 1969), p. 98.

literally as big as a house. The looms used by weavers expanded from small machines that fitted into the cottages of artisan-weavers to monstrous mechanisms housed in mills that still impress us by their size.

Equally remarkable was the expansion in the social scale of production. The new technology almost immediately outstripped the administrative capability of the small-sized business establishment. As the apparatus of production increased in size, it also increased in speed. As outputs grew from rivulets to rivers, a much larger organization was needed to manage production—to arrange for the steady arrival of raw materials, to supervise the work process, and not least, to find a market for its end product.

Thus, we find the size of the typical business enterprise steadily increasing as its technological basis became more complex. In the last quarter of the eighteenth century a factory of ten persons was worthy of note by Adam Smith, as we shall see in our next chapter. By the first quarter of the nineteenth century an ordinary textile mill employed several hundred men and women. Fifty years later many railways employed as many individuals as constituted the armies of respectable monarchs in Adam Smith's time. And in still another fifty years, by the 1920s, large manufacturing companies had almost as many employees as the populations of eighteenth-century cities.

Technology also played a decisive role in changing the nature of that most basic of all human activities, work. It did so by breaking down the complicated tasks of productive activity into much smaller subtasks, many of which could then be duplicated, or at least greatly assisted, by mechanical contrivances. This process was called the division of labor. Adam Smith was soon to explain, as we shall see, that the division of labor was mainly responsible for the increase in productivity of the average worker.

The division of labor altered social life in other ways as well. Work became more fragmented, monotonous, tedious, alienated. And the self-sufficiency of individuals was curtailed greatly. In precapitalist days most people either directly produced their own subsistence or made some article that could be exchanged for subsistence: peasants grew crops; artisans produced cloth, shoes, implements. But as work became more and more finely divided, the products of work became ever smaller pieces of the total jigsaw puzzle. Individuals did not spin thread or weave cloth, but manipulated levers and fed the machinery that did the actual spinning or weaving. A worker in a shoe plant made uppers or lowers or heels, but not shoes. No one of these jobs, performed by itself, would have sustained its performer for a single day; and no one of these products could have been exchanged for another product except through the complicated market network. Technology freed men and women from much material want, but it bound them to the workings of the market mechanism.

Not least of the mighty impacts of technology was its exposure of men and women to an unprecedented degree of change. Some of this was welcome, for change literally opened new horizons of material life: travel, for instance, once the prerogative of the wealthy, became a possibility for the masses, as the flood of nineteenth-century immigration to the United States revealed.

However, the changes introduced by technology had their negative side as well. Already buffeted by market forces that could mysteriously dry up the need for work or just as mysteriously create it, society now discovered that entire occupations, skills acquired over a lifetime, companies laboriously built up over generations, age-old industries could be threatened by the appearance of technological change. Increasingly, productive machinery appeared as the enemy, rather than the ally, of humankind. By the early nineteenth century the textile weavers, whose cottage industry was destroyed gradually by competition from the mills, were banding together to burn down the hated buildings.

These aspects of change do not begin to exhaust the ways in which technology, coupled with the market system, altered the very meaning of existence. But in considering them, we see how profound and how wrenching was the revolution that capitalism introduced. Technology was a genie that capitalism let out of the bottle; it has ever since refused to go back in.

THE POLITICAL DIMENSION

The disturbing, upsetting, revolutionary nature of the market and technology sets the stage for one last aspect of capitalism that we want to note: the political currents of change that capitalism brought, as much a part of the history of capitalism as the emergence of the market or the dismantling of the barriers against technical change.

One of these political currents was the rise of democratic, or parliamentary, institutions. Democratic political institutions far predate capitalism, as the history of ancient Athens or the Icelandic medieval parliamentary system shows. Nonetheless, the rise of the mercantile classes was closely tied to the struggle against the privileges and legal institutions of European feudalism. The historic movement that eventually swept aside the precapitalist economic order also swept aside its political order. Along with the emergence of the market system we find a parallel and supporting emergence of more open political ways of life.

We must resist the temptation of claiming that capitalism either guarantees, or is necessary for, political freedom. We have seen some capitalist nations, such as pre-Hitler Germany, descend into totalitarian dictatorship. We have seen other nations, such as Sweden, move toward a kind of social-minded capitalism without impairing democratic liberties. Moreover, the exercise of political democracy was very limited in early capitalism: Adam Smith, for example, although comfortably off, did not possess enough property to allow him to vote.

It is true, to be sure, that political liberties did not exist or scarcely existed in communist nations that have deliberately sought to remove the market system. This suggests, although it does not prove, that some vital connection exists between democratic privileges as we know them and an open society of economic contract, whether it be formally capitalist or not.

Because of the economic freedom on which the market system has always rested, the basic philosophy of capitalism from Adam Smith's day forward has been laissez-faire—leaving things alone.* As we study economics further, we will be tracing the evolution of that idea—the idea of leaving the market alone—as well as investigating what has happened to the system, both when it was left alone and when it wasn't.

It is much too early to take up that controversy here. Suffice it to say that if capitalism brought a strong impetus for laissez-faire, it also brought a strong impetus for economic intervention. The very democratic liberties and political equalities that were encouraged by the rise of capitalism became powerful forces that sought to curb or change the manner in which the economic system worked. Indeed, within a few years of Adam Smith's time, the idea of leaving things alone was al-

---

*It is said that a group of merchants called on the great Colbert, French finance minister from 1661 to 1683, who congratulated them on their contribution to the French economy and asked what he could do for them. The answer was *"Laissez-nous faire"*—leave us alone. Since Colbert was a strong proponent of the complex regulations and red tape that tied up industry in France at this time, we can imagine how gladly he received this advice.

ready breached by the English Factory Act of 1833, establishing a system of inspectors to prevent child and female labor from being abused. In our own day that same political desire to correct the unhampered workings of laissez-faire capitalism has given rise to the Social Security system, which provides a social floor beneath the market, and to the environmental legislation that limits the market's operation in certain areas.

Thus, from the beginning, capitalism has been characterized by a tension between laissez-faire and intervention—laissez-faire representing the expression of its economic drive, intervention its democratic political orientation. That tension continues today, a deeply imbedded part of the historic character of the capitalist system.

TWO

Three Great Economists

A look back over economic history has taught us something about capitalism, the social system with which economics is mainly concerned. But we have not yet gained a sense of what economics itself is about. Perhaps we can see, however, that economics is mainly "about" capitalism—that it is an effort to explain how a society knit together by the market rather than by tradition or command, powered by a restive technology rather than by inertia, could hang together, how it would work.

There is no better way of grasping this basic purpose of economics than to look at the work of three great economists—Adam Smith, Karl Marx, and John Maynard Keynes. The three names raise blood pressures differently, depending on whether one is a conservative, a radical, or a liberal. That's a matter for a different kind of book than this one. We want to explain what Smith, Marx, and Keynes *saw* when they looked at capitalism, for their visions still define the field of economics for everyone, right and left alike.

ADAM SMITH (1723–1790)

Adam Smith is the patron saint of our discipline and a figure of towering intellectual stature. His fame resides in his masterpiece, which everyone has heard of and almost no one has read, *The Wealth of Nations,* published in 1776, the year of the Declaration of Independence. All things considered, it is not easy to say which document is of greater historic importance. The Declaration sounded a new call for society dedicated to "Life, Liberty, and the pursuit of Happiness." The *Wealth* explained how such a society worked.

Here Smith begins by addressing a perplexing question. The actors in the market, as we know, are all driven by the desire to make money for themselves—to "better their condition," as Smith puts it. The problem is obvious. How does a market society prevent self-interested, profit-hungry individuals from holding up their fellow citizens for ransom? How can a socially workable arrangement arise from such a dangerously unsocial motivation as self-betterment?

The answer introduces us to a central mechanism of a market system, the mechanism of competition. Each person out for self-betterment, with no thought of others, is faced with a host of similarly motivated persons. As a result, each market actor, in buying or selling, is forced to meet the prices offered by competitors.

In the kind of competition that Smith assumes, a manufacturer who tries to charge more than other manufacturers will not be able to find any buyers. A job seeker who asks more than the going wage will not be able to find work. And an employer who tries to pay less than competitors pay will not find workers to fill the jobs. In this way, the market mechanism imposes a discipline on its participants—buyers must bid against other buyers and therefore cannot gang up against sellers. Sellers must contend against other sellers and therefore cannot impose their will on buyers.

But the market has a second, equally important function. Smith shows that the market will arrange for the production of the goods that society wants, in the quantities society wants—without anyone ever issuing an order of any kind. Suppose that consumers want more pots and fewer pans than are being turned out. The public will buy up the existing stock of pots, and as a result their prices will rise. Contrariwise, the pan business will be dull; as pan makers try to get rid of their inventories, pan prices will fall.

Now a restorative force comes into play. As pot prices rise, so will profits in the pot business; and as pan prices fall, so will profits in that business. Once again, the drive for self-betterment will go to work. Employers in the favored pot business will seek to expand, hiring more factors of production—more workers, more space, more capital equipment; and employers in the disfavored pan business will reduce their use of the factors of production, letting workers go, giving up leases on space, cutting down on their capital investment.

PORTRAIT OF AN ABSENTMINDED PROFESSOR

"I am a beau in nothing but my books" was the way that Adam Smith once described himself. Indeed, a famous medallion profile shows us a homely face. In addition, Smith had a curious stumbling gait that one friend called vermicular and was given to notorious fits of absentmindedness. On one occasion, absorbed in discussion, he fell into a tanning pit.

Few other adventures befell Smith in the course of his scholarly, rather retiring life. Perhaps the high point was reached at age four when he was kidnapped by a band of gypsies passing near Kirkaidy, his native hamlet in Scotland. His captors held him only a few hours; they may have sensed what a biographer later wrote: "He would have made, I fear, a poor gypsy."

Marked out early as a student of promise, at sixteen Smith won a scholarship that sent him to Oxford. But Oxford was not then the center of learning that it is today. Little or no systematic teaching took place, the students being free to educate themselves, provided they did not read dangerous books. Smith was nearly expelled for owning a copy of David Hume's *Treatise of Human Nature,* a work we now regard as one of the philosophic masterpieces of the eighteenth century.

After Oxford, Smith returned to Scotland, where he obtained an appointment as professor of moral philosophy at the University of Glasgow. Moral philosophy covered a large territory in Smith's time. We have notes of his lectures in which he talked about jurisprudence, military organization, taxation, and "police"—the last word meaning the administration of domestic affairs that we would call economic policy.

In 1759 Smith published *The Theory of Moral Sentiments,* a remarkable inquiry into morality and psychology. The book attracted widespread attention and brought Smith to the notice of Lord Townshend, one day to be the Chancellor of the Exchequer, responsible for the notorious tax on American tea. Townshend engaged Smith to serve as tutor to his stepson, and Smith resigned his professional post to set off on the grand tour with his charge. In France he met Voltaire, Rousseau, and François Quesnay, the brilliant doctor who had originated the ideas of physiocracy, a pioneering attempt to explain how the economic system functioned. Smith would have dedicated *The Wealth of Nations* to him, had Quesnay not died.

Returning to Scotland in 1766, Smith lived out the remainder of his life largely in scholarly retirement. It was during these years that the *Wealth* was slowly and carefully composed. When it was done, Smith sent a copy to David Hume, by then his dear friend. Hume wrote: "Euge!* Belle! Dear Mr. Smith: I am much pleased with your Performance. . . ." Hume knew, as did virtually everyone who read the book, that Smith had written a work that would permanently change society's understanding of itself.

---

* "Well done!"

Hence the output of pots will rise and that of pans will fall. And this is what the public wanted in the first place. The pressures of the marketplace direct the selfish activities of individuals as if by an Invisible Hand (to use Smith's wonderful phrase) into socially responsible paths. Thus the workings of the competitive system transmute self-regarding behavior into socially useful outcomes. The Invisible Hand—the words that describe the overall process—keeps society on track, assuring that it produces the goods and services it needs.

Smith's demonstration of how a market performs this extraordinary feat has never ceased to be of interest. Much of economics, as we shall see in closer detail later, is concerned with scrutinizing carefully how the Invisible Hand works. Not that it always does work. There are areas of economic life where the Invisible Hand does not exert its influence at all. In every market system, for instance, tradition continues to play a role in nonmarket methods of remuneration such as tipping. So, too, command is always in evidence within businesses, for example in hiring or firing, or in the exercise of government powers such as taxation. Further, the market system has no way of providing certain public goods—goods that cannot be privately marketed, such as national defense or public law and order. Smith knew about these and recognized that such goods would have to be supplied by the government. Then, too, the market does not always meet the ethical or aesthetic criteria of society, or it may produce goods that are profitable to make but harmful to consume. We shall look into these problems in due course. At this juncture, however, we had better stand in considerable awe of Smith's basic insight, for he showed his generation and all succeeding ones that a market system is a powerful force for orderly social provisioning.

He also showed that it was self-regulating. The beautiful consequence of the market is that it is its own guardian. If anyone's prices, wages, or profits stray from levels that are set for everyone, the force of competition will drive them back. Thus a curious paradox exists. The market, which is the acme of economic freedom, turns out to be the strictest of economic taskmasters. One can always appeal to a king for a special dispensation. There is no appeal to the market.

Because the market is its own regulator, Smith was opposed to government intervention that would interfere with the workings of self-interest and competition. Therefore laissez-faire became his fundamental philosophy, as it remains the fundamental philosophy of conservative-minded economists today. His commitment to the Invisible Hand did not make Smith a conventional conservative, however. He is cautious about, not dead set against, government intervention. Moreover, *The Wealth of Nations* is shot through with biting remarks about the "mean and rapacious" ways of the manufacturing class, and openly sympathetic with the lot of the workingman, hardly a popular position in Smith's day. What ultimately makes Smith a conservative—and here he *is* in accord with modern views—is his belief that the system of "natural liberty" founded on economic freedom would ultimately benefit the general public.

Needless to say, that is a question to which we will return many times. But we are not yet done with Adam Smith. For matching his remarkable vision of an internally coherent market system was an equally new and remarkable vision of another kind. Smith saw that the system of "natural liberty"—the market system, left to its own devices—would grow, that the wealth of such a nation would steadily increase.

What brought about this growth? As before, the motive force was the drive for self-betterment, the thirst for profits, the wish to make money. This meant that every employer was constantly seeking to accumulate more capital, to expand the wealth of the enterprise; in turn, this led each employer to seek to increase sales in the hope of gaining a larger profit.

But how to enlarge sales in a day long before advertising existed as we know it? Smith's answer was to improve productivity: Increase the output of the work force. And the road to increasing productivity was very clear: Improve the division of labor.

In Smith's conception of the growing wealth (we would say the growing *production*) of nations, the division of labor therefore plays a central role, as this famous description of a pin factory makes unforgettably clear:

> One man draws out the wire, another straits it, a third cuts it, a fourth points it, a fifth grinds it at the top for receiving the head; to make the head requires two or three distinct operations; to put it on is a peculiar business; to whiten it another; it is even a trade by itself to put them into paper. . . .
>
> I have seen a small manufactory of this kind where ten men only were employed and where some of them consequently performed two or three distinct operations. But though they were poor, and therefore but indifferently accommodated with the necessary machinery, they could when they exerted themselves make among them about twelve pounds of pins in a day. There are in a pound upwards of four thousand pins of middling size. These ten persons, therefore, could make among them upwards of forty-eight thousand pins in a day. . . . But if they had all wrought separately and independently . . . they could certainly not each of them make twenty, perhaps not one pin in a day.*

How is the division of labor to be enhanced? Smith places principal importance on the manner already announced in his description of the process of making pins: Organization is the key. In addition, the division of labor—and therefore the productivity of labor—is increased when the tasks of production can be taken over, or aided and assisted, by the capacities of machinery. In this way each firm seeking to expand is naturally led to introduce more machinery as a way of improving the productivity of its workers. *Thereby the market system becomes an immense force for the accumulation of capital, mainly in the form of machinery and equipment.*

Moreover, Smith showed something remarkable about the self-regulating properties of the market system as a growth-producing institution. We recall that growth occurred because employers installed machinery that improved the division of labor. But as they thereupon added to their work force, would it not follow that wages would rise as all employers competed to hire labor? And would that not squeeze profits and dry up the funds with which machinery could be bought?

Once again, however, the market was its own regulator. For Smith showed that the increased *demand* for labor would be matched by an

*Adam Smith, *The Wealth of Nations* (New York: Modern Library, 1937), pp. 4, 5.

increased *supply* of labor, so that wages would not rise or would rise only moderately. The reason was plausible. In Smith's day, infant and child mortality rates were horrendous: "It is not uncommon," wrote Smith, ". . . in the Highlands of Scotland for a mother who has borne twenty children not to have two alive." As wages rose and better food was provided for the household, infant and child mortality would decline. Soon there would be a larger work force available for hire: ten was the working age in Smith's day. The larger work force would hold back the rise in wages—and so the accumulation of capital could go on. Just as the system assured its short-term viability of self-regulating the output of pots and pans, so it assured its long-term viability by self-regulating its steady growth.

Of course, Smith wrote about a world that is long since vanished—a world in which a factory of ten people, although small, was still significant enough to mention; in which remnants of mercantilist, and even feudal, restrictions determined how many apprentices an employer could hire in many trades; in which labor unions were largely illegal; in which almost no social legislation existed; and above all, where the great majority of people were very poor.

Yet Smith saw two essential attributes in the economic system that was not yet fully born at that time: first, that a society of competitive, profit-seeking individuals can assure its orderly material provisioning through the self-regulating market mechanism; and second, that such a society tends to accumulate capital, and in so doing, to enhance its productivity and wealth. These insights are not the last word. We have already mentioned that the market mechanism does not always work successfully, and our next two economists will demonstrate that the growth process is not without serious defects. But the insights themselves are still germane. What is surprising after two centuries is not how mistaken Smith was, but how deeply he saw. In a real sense, as economists we are still his pupils.

KARL MARX (1818–1883)

To most Americans, Karl Marx's name conjures up revolutionary images. To a certain extent, that is perfectly correct (see box on page 34). But for our purposes, Marx is much more than a political activist. He was a profoundly penetrative economic thinker, perhaps the most remarkable analyst of capitalism's dynamics who ever lived. So we will spend no time at all defending or assailing his political philosophy. What interests us is what he saw in capitalism that was different from Smith.

Adam Smith was the analyst of capitalism's orderliness and progress. Oddly enough, he failed to see the regenerative inventiveness of the new technology of industry—which, in all fairness, was still in its infancy during his lifetime. Smith actually believed that after a time a Society of Perfect Liberty would accumulate all the capital for which it had a need, after which it would go into a deep decline! As to what might happen next, he said nothing.* Marx was the diagnostician of its disorders and eventual demise. Their differences are rooted in the fundamentally opposite way that each saw history. In Smith's view, history was a succession of stages through which humankind traveled, climbing from the "early and rude" society of hunters and fisherfolk to the final stage of commercial society. Marx saw history as a continuing struggle among social classes, ruling classes contending with ruled classes in every era.

Moreover, Smith believed that commercial society would bring about a harmonious, mutually acceptable solution to the problem of individual interest in a social setting that would go on forever—or at least for a very long time. Marx saw tension and antagonism as the outcome of the class struggle, and the setting of capitalist society as anything but permanent. Indeed, the class struggle, expressed as the contest over wages and profits, would be the main force for changing capitalism and eventually undoing it.

A great deal of interest in Marx's work focuses on that revolutionary perspective and purpose. But Marx the economist interests us for a different reason: Marx also saw the market as a powerful force in the accumulation of capital and wealth. From his conflict-laden point of view, however, he traces out the process—mainly in Volume II of *Capital*—quite differently than Smith does. As we have seen, Smith's conception of the growth process stressed its self-regulatory nature, its steady, hitch-free path. Marx's conception is just the opposite. To him, growth is a process full of pitfalls, a process in which crisis or malfunction lurks at every turn.

Marx starts with a view of the accumulation process that is much

*Wealth of Nations, pp. 94–95.

PROFILE OF A REVOLUTIONARY

A great, bearded, dark-complected man, Karl Marx was the picture of a revolutionary. And he was one—engaged, mind and heart, in the effort to overthrow the system of capitalism that he spent his whole life studying. As a political revolutionary, Marx was not very successful, although with his lifelong friend Friedrich Engels, he formed an international working class "movement" that frightened a good many conservative governments. But as an intellectual revolutionary Marx was surely among the most successful disturbers of thought who ever lived; at least until the rise and collapse of the Soviet Union.

Marx led as turbulent and active a life as Smith's was secluded and academic. Born to middle-class parents in Trier, Germany, Marx was marked early as a student of prodigious abilities, but not temperamentally cut out to be a professor. Soon after getting his doctoral degree (in philosophy) Marx became editor of a crusading, but not communist, newspaper, which rapidly earned the distrust of the reactionary Prussian government. It closed down the paper. Typically, Marx printed the last edition in red. With his wife, Jenny (and Jenny's family maid, Lenchen, who remained with them, unpaid, all her life), Marx thereupon began life as a political exile in Paris, Brussels, and finally in London. There, in 1848, together with Engels, he published the pamphlet that was to become his best known but certainly not most important work: *The Communist Manifesto.*

The remainder of Marx's life was lived in London. Terribly poor, largely as a consequence of his hopeless inability to manage his own finances, Marx's life was spent in the reading room of the British Museum, laboriously composing the great, never-finished opus, *Capital.* No economist has ever read so widely or so deeply as Marx. Before even beginning *Capital,* he wrote a profound three-volume commentary on all the existing economists, eventually published as *Theories of Surplus Value,* and filled thirty-seven notebooks on subjects that would be included in *Capital*—these notes, published as the *Grundrisse* (Foundations) did not appear in print until 1953. *Capital* itself was written backwards, first Volumes II and III, in very rough draft form, then Volume I, the only part of the great opus that appeared in Marx's lifetime, in 1867.

Despite the fall of Soviet communism, Marx was assuredly a man who altered every aspect of thinking about society—historical and sociological as well as economic—as decisively as Plato altered the cast of philosophic thought or Freud that of psychology. Very few economists today work their way through the immense body of Marx's work, but in one way or another his influence affects most of us, even if we are unaware of it. We owe to Marx the basic idea that capitalism is an *evolving* system, deriving from a specific historic past and moving slowly and irregularly toward a dimly discernible, different form of society. That is an idea accepted by many social scientists who may or may not approve of socialism, and who are on the whole vehemently "anti-Marxist."

---

like that of a businessman. The problem is how to make a given sum of capital—money sitting in a bank or invested in a firm—yield a profit. As Marx puts it, how does M (a sum of money) become M', a *larger* sum?

Marx's answer begins with capitalists using their money to buy commodities and labor power. Thereby they make ready the process of production, obtaining needed raw or semifinished materials, and hiring the working capabilities of a labor force. Here the possibility for crisis lies in the difficulty that capitalists may have in getting their materials or their labor force at the right price. If that should happen—if labor is too expensive, for instance—M stays put and the accumulation process never gets started at all.

But suppose the first stage of accumulation takes place smoothly. Now money capital has been transformed into a hired work force and a stock of physical goods. These have next to be combined in the labor process; that is, actual work must be expended on the materials, and the raw or semifinished goods transformed into their next stage of production.

It is here, on the factory floor, that Marx sees the genesis of profit. In his view, profit lies in the ability of capitalists to pay less for labor power—for the working abilities of their work force—than the actual value workers will impart to the commodities they help to produce. Thus, profit—the difference between M and M'—essentially resides in underpaid labor. This theory of *surplus value* as the source of profit is very important in Marx's analysis of capitalism, but it is not central to our purpose here. Instead, we stop only to note that the labor process is another place where accumulation can be disrupted. If there is a strike, or if production encounters snags, the money capital (M) that is invested in goods and labor power will not move along toward its objective, a larger sum of money capital (M').

But once again suppose that all goes well and workers transform steel sheets, rubber casings, and bolts of cloth into automobiles. The automobiles are not yet money. They have to be sold—and here, of course, lie the familiar problems of the marketplace: bad guesses as to the public's taste; mismatches between supply and demand; recessions that diminish the spending power of society.

If all goes well, the commodities *will* be sold—and sold for M', which is bigger than M. In that case, the circuit of accumulation is complete, and the capitalists will have a new sum M', which they will want to spend on another round, hoping to win M''. But unlike Adam Smith's smooth-growth model, we can see that Marx's conception of accumulation is riddled with pitfalls and dangers. Crisis is possible at every stage. Indeed, in the complex theory that Marx unfolds in *Capital,* the inherent tendency of the system is to generate crisis, not to avoid it.

We will not trace Marx's theory of capitalism further except to note that at its core lies a complicated analysis of the manner in which surplus value (the unpaid labor that is the source of profit) is squeezed out through mechanization. Someone who wants to learn about Marx's analysis must turn to other books, of which there are many.*

Our interest lies in Marx as the first theorist to stress the instability of capitalism. Adam Smith originated the idea that growth is an inherent characteristic of capitalism, but to Marx we owe the idea that that growth is wavering and uncertain, far from the assured process Smith described. Marx makes it clear that capital accumulation must overcome the uncertainty inherent in the market system and the tension of

---

*At the risk of appearing self-serving, a useful introduction is R. L. Heilbroner, *Marxism: For and Against* (New York: Norton, 1980).

the opposing demands of labor and capital. The accumulation of wealth, although always the objective of business, may not always be within its power to achieve.

In *Capital*, Marx sees instability increasing until finally the system comes tumbling down. His reasoning involves two further, very important prognoses for the system. The first is that *the size of business firms will steadily increase as the consequence of the recurrent crises that rack the economy*. With each crisis, small firms go bankrupt and their assets are bought up by surviving firms. A trend toward big business is therefore an integral part of capitalism.

Second, *Marx expects an intensification of the class struggle as the result of the "proletarianization" of the labor force*. More and more small business people and independent artisans will be squeezed out in the crisis-ridden process of growth. Thus the social structure will be reduced to two classes—a small group of capitalist magnates and a large mass of proletarianized (i.e., propertyless), embittered workers.

In the end, this situation proves impossible to maintain. In Marx's words:

> Along with the constant decrease in the number of capitalist magnates, who usurp and monopolize all the advantages of this process of transformation, the mass of misery, oppression, slavery, degradation and exploitation grows; but with this there also grows the revolt of the working class, a class constantly increasing in numbers, and trained, united and organized by the very mechanism of the capitalist process of production. The monopoly of capital becomes a fetter upon the mode of production which has flourished alongside and under it. The centralization of the means of production and the socialization of labour reach a point at which they become incompatible with their capitalist integument. This integument is burst asunder. The knell of capitalist private property sounds. The expropriators are expropriated.*

Much of the economic controversy that Marx generated has been focused on the questions: Will capitalism ultimately undo itself? Will its internal tensions, its "contradictions," as Marx calls them, finally become too much for its market mechanism to handle?

There are no simple answers to these questions. Critics of Marx vehemently insist that capitalism has *not* collapsed, that the working class

---

*Karl Marx, *Capital*, Vol. I (New York: Vintage, 1977), p. 929.

has *not* become more and more miserable, and that a number of predictions Marx made, such as that the rate of profit would tend to decline, have not been verified.

Supporters of Marx argue the opposite case. They stress that capitalism almost did collapse in the 1930s. They note that more and more people have been reduced to a "proletarian" status, working for a capitalist firm rather than for themselves; in 1800, for example, 80 percent of Americans were self-employed; today the figure is less than 10 percent. They stress that the size of business has constantly grown, and that Marx did correctly foresee that the capitalist system itself would expand, pushing into noncapitalist Asia, South America, and Africa.

It is doubtful that Marx's contribution as a social analyst will ultimately be determined by this kind of scorecard. Certainly he made many remarkably penetrating statements; equally certainly, he said things about the prospects for capitalism that seem to have been wrong. Most economists do not accept Marx's diagnosis of class struggle as the great motor of change in capitalist and precapitalist societies or his prognosis of a trend toward socialism. But what Marx's reputation ultimately rests on is something else. It rests on his vision of capitalism as a system under tension, and in a process of continuous evolution as a consequence of that tension. Few would deny the validity of that vision.

There is much more to Marx than the few economic ideas sketched here. Indeed, Marx should not be thought of primarily as an economist, but as a pioneer in a new kind of critical social thought: It is significant that the subtitle of *Capital* is *A Critique of Political Economy*.

In the gallery of the world's great thinkers, where Marx unquestionably belongs, his proper place is with historians rather than economists. Most appropriately, his statue would be centrally placed, overlooking many corridors of thought—sociological analysis, philosophic inquiry, and of course, economics.

For Marx's lasting contribution was a penetration of the *appearances* of our social system and of the ways in which we think about that system, in an effort to arrive at buried essences deep below the surface. That most searching aspect of Marx's work is not one we will pursue here, but bear it in mind, because it accounts for the persisting interest of Marx's thought.

Finally, what about the relation of Marx to present-day communism?

That is a subject for a book about the politics, not the economics, of Marxism. Marx himself was a fervent democrat—but a very intolerant man. More important, his system of ideas has also been intolerant, and may thereby have encouraged intolerance in revolutionary parties that have based their ideas on his thought. Marx himself died long before Soviet communism rose and fell. We cannot know what he would have made of it—probably he would have been horrified at its excesses but still hopeful for some kind of democratic socialism in the future.

Here a parting thought may help sum up this complex and certainly seminal thinker. To no small degree, Marx's analytic penetration was based on his insistence that the economy was the "base" of society, whence his energies arose, and that the political and social framework was but a "superstructure" where these energies would exert their influence. This came as a galvanizing view at a time when most social observers looked to politics as the driving force of society and relegated the economy to a relatively secondary place.

But in our times we have come to see that Marx's view, however perceptive in "normal" times, can be a source of misperception in critical periods. The hideous lesson of the self-demolition of Yugoslavia, of the Soviet Union's meltdown, and of central Africa's ferocious ethnic hostilities indicates that there is a subbasement beneath Marx's base—a place where political and social passions may slumber for decades but erupt with terrific force when a spark strikes the wrong place. If there is any one reason why Marxism has lost much of its once powerful intellectual magnetism, it is the rediscovery of the lurking power of political and social beliefs, perhaps the most disconcerting lesson of our time for economists.

JOHN MAYNARD KEYNES* (1883–1946)

Marx was the intellectual prophet of capitalism as a self-destructive system; John Maynard Keynes was the engineer of capitalism repaired. Today, that is not an uncontested statement. To some people, Keynes's doctrines are as dangerous and subversive as those of Marx—a curious irony, since Keynes himself was totally opposed to Marxist thought and wholly in favor of sustaining and improving the capitalist system.

*This is probably the most mispronounced name in economics. It should be pronounced "canes," not "keens."

The reason for the continuing distrust of Keynes is that more than any other economist, he is the father of the idea of a "mixed economy" in which the government plays a crucial role. To many people these days, all government activities are suspicious at best and downright injurious at worst. Thus, in some quarters Keynes's name is under a cloud. Nonetheless, he remains one of the great innovators of our discipline, a mind to be ranked with Smith and Marx as one of the most influential our profession has brought forth. As Nobelist Milton Friedman, an avowed conservative, has declared: "We are all Keynesians now."

The great economists were all products of their times: Smith, the voice of optimistic, nascent capitalism; Marx, the spokesman for the victims of its bleakest industrial period; Keynes, the product of a still later time, the Great Depression.

PORTRAIT OF A MANY-SIDED ENGLISHMAN

Keynes was certainly a man of many talents. Unlike Smith or Marx, he was at home in the world of business affairs, a shrewd dealer and financier. Every morning, abed, he would scan the newspaper and make his commitments for the day on the most treacherous of all markets, foreign exchange. An hour or so a day sufficed to make him a very rich man; only the great English economist David Ricardo (1772–1823) could match him in financial acumen. Like Ricardo, Keynes was a speculator by temperament. During World War I, when he was at the Treasury office running England's foreign currency operations, he reported with glee to his chief that he had got together a fair amount of Spanish pesetas. The chief was relieved that England had a supply of *that* currency for a while. "Oh no," said Keynes. "I've sold them all. I'm going to break the market." And he did. Later during the war, when the Germans were shelling Paris, he went to France to negotiate for the English government; on the side, he bought some marvelous French masterpieces at much reduced prices for the National Gallery—along with a Cézanne for himself.

More than an economist and speculator, he was a brilliant mathematician; a businessman who very successfully ran a great investment trust; a ballet lover who married a famous ballerina; a superb stylist and an editor of consummate skill; a man of huge kindness when he wanted to exert it, and of ferocious wit when (more often) he chose to exert that. On one occasion, banker Sir Harry Goshen criticized Keynes for not "letting things take their natural course." "Is it more appropriate to smile or rage at these artless sentiments?" wrote Keynes. "Best, perhaps, to let Sir Harry take *his* natural course."

Keynes's greatest fame lay in his economic inventiveness. He came by this talent naturally enough as the son of a distinguished economist, John Neville Keynes. As an undergraduate, Keynes had already attracted the attention of Alfred Marshall, the commanding figure at Cambridge University for three decades. After graduation, Keynes soon won notice with a brilliant little book on Indian finance; he then became an adviser to the English government in the negotiations at the end of World War I. Dismayed and disheartened by the vengeful terms of the Versailles Treaty, Keynes wrote a brilliant polemic, *The Economic Consequences of the Peace,* which won him international renown.

Almost thirty years later, Keynes would himself be a chief negotiator for the English government, first in securing the necessary loans during World War II, then as one of the architects of the Bretton Woods agreement that opened a new system of international currency relations after that war. On his return home from one trip to Washington, reporters crowded around to ask if England had been sold out and would soon be another American state. Keynes's reply was succinct: "No such luck."

The Depression hit America like a typhoon. One half the value of all production simply disappeared. One quarter of the working force lost its jobs. Over a million urban families found their mortgages foreclosed, their houses lost to them. Nine million savings accounts went down the drain when banks closed, many for good.

Against this terrible reality of joblessness and loss of income, the economics profession, like the business world or government advisers, had nothing to offer. Fundamentally, economists were as perplexed at the behavior of the economy as were the American people themselves. In many ways the situation reminds us of the uncertainty that the public and the economics profession have shared in the face of inflation in modern times.

It was against this setting of dismay and near-panic that Keynes's great book appeared: *The General Theory of Employment, Interest and Money.* A complicated book—much more technical than *The Wealth of Nations* or *Capital*—the *General Theory* nevertheless had a central message that was simple enough to grasp. The overall level of economic activity in a capitalist system, said Keynes (and Marx and Adam Smith would have agreed with him) was determined by the willingness of its entrepreneurs to make capital investments. From time to time this willingness was blocked by considerations that made capital accumulation difficult or impossible: In Smith's model we saw the possibility of wages rising too fast, and Marx's theory pointed out difficulties at every stage of the process.

But all the previous economists—even Marx, to a certain extent—believed that a failure to accumulate capital would be a temporary, self-curing setback. In Smith's scheme, the rising supply of young workers would keep wages in check. In Marx's conception, each crisis (up to the last) would present the surviving entrepreneurs with fresh opportunities to resume their quest for profits. For Keynes, however, the diagnosis was more severe. He showed that a market system could reach a position of "under-employment equilibrium"—a kind of steady, stagnant state—despite the presence of unemployed workers and unused industrial equipment. *The revolutionary import of Keynes's theory was that there was no self-correcting property in the market system to keep capitalism growing.*

We will understand the nature of Keynes's diagnosis better after we have studied a little more economics, but we can easily see the conclusion to which his diagnosis drove him. If there was nothing that would automatically provide for capital accumulation, a badly depressed economy could remain in the doldrums unless some substitute were found for business capital spending. And there was only one such possible source of stimulation. This was the government. The crux of Keynes's message was therefore that government spending might be an essential economic policy for a depressed capitalism trying to recover its vitality.

Whether or not Keynes's remedy works and what consequences government spending may have for a market system have become major topics for contemporary economics—topics we will deal with later at length. But we can see the significance of Keynes's work in changing the very conception of the economic system in which we live. Adam

Smith's view of the market system led to the philosophy of laissez-faire, allowing the system to generate its own natural propensity for growth and internal order. Marx stressed a very different view, in which instability and crisis lurked at every stage, but of course Marx was not interested in policies to maintain capitalism. Keynes propounded a philosophy as far removed from Marx as from Smith. For if Keynes was right, laissez-faire was not the appropriate policy for capitalism—certainly not for capitalism in depression. And if Keynes was right about his remedy, the gloomy prognostications of Marx were also incorrect—or at least could be rendered incorrect.

But was Keynes right? Was Smith right? Was Marx right? To a very large degree these questions frame the subject matter of economics today. That is why, even if their theories are part of our history, the "worldly philosophers" are also contemporary. A young writer once remarked impatiently to T. S. Eliot that it seemed so pointless to study the thinkers of the past, because we know so much more than they. "Yes," replied Eliot. "They are what we know."

THREE

A Bird's-Eye View of the Economy

We are almost, but not quite, ready to begin to learn modern economics. The trouble is that we can't begin to study economics without knowing something about the economy. But what is "the economy"? When we turn to the economics section of *Time* or *Newsweek* or pick up a business magazine, a jumble of things meets the eye: stock market ups and downs, reports on company fortunes and mishaps, accounts of incomprehensible "fluctuations in the exchange market," columns by business pundits, stories about unemployment or globalization.

How much of this is relevant? How are we to make our way through this barrage of reporting to something that we can identify as the economy?

THE TWO WORLDS OF BUSINESS

Of course, we know where to start. Business enterprise is the very heart of an economic system of private property and market relationships. Let us begin, then, with a look at the world of business.*

---

*A word of caution here: Most of the statistics that follow will not be those of last year or even the year before. This is because it takes takes two to three years before most economic data are considered reliable enough to become part of our official statistics. Fortunately, the figures that interest us in this chapter do not change radically from one year to the next—they are meant to give us orders of magnitude rather than exact values.

The following table makes one thing immediately clear: There are at least two worlds of business. One of them, mainly proprietorships (businesses owned by a single person) and partnerships, is the world of very small business—businesses that gross less than $100,000 a year. Of course there are a tiny corporations, too, and there are some very big proprietorships and partnerships. But the main thing is the smallness. Here we find the bulk of the firms that fill the Yellow Pages of the phone book, the great preponderance of the country's farms, myriad mom-and-pop stores, restaurants, motels, dry cleaners, druggists, retailers—in short, over 75 percent of all the business firms in the nation.

DIMENSIONS OF BUSINESS, 1993*

	Total number of firms (000's omitted)	Total sales (billions)	Average sales per firm
Proprietorships (non-farm)	15,848	$ 757	$ 47,766
Partnerships	1,468	627	427,112
Corporations	3,765	11,814	2,979,570

* This and nearly all subsequent data from *Statistical Abstract of the United States,* Dept. of Commerce, Washington, D.C., 1994, p. 519.

Small business is the part of the business world with which we are all most familiar. We understand how a hardware store is run, whereas we have only vague ideas about how General Motors or IBM operates. But the world of small business warrants our attention for two other reasons. First, small business is the employer of a substantial fraction—about one quarter—of the nation's labor force. Second, because the small-business proprietary point of view directly expresses the socioeconomic position of about one married household out of every five, the world of small business is the source of much middle-class opinion.

Meanwhile, we have already glimpsed another business world, mainly to be found in the corporate enterprises of the nation. Compare the average size of the sales of corporations with those of proprietorships and partnerships: the ratio is well over 50 to 1 for proprietorships; and almost 10 to 1 for partnerships. But even these figures hide the extraordinary difference between very big business and small business.

Within the world of corporations roughly 80 percent do less than $1 million worth of business a year. But the 17-odd percent that do more than $1 million worth take in almost 95 percent of the receipts of all corporations.

Thus, counterposed to a world of very numerous small businesses, there is the world of much-less-numerous big businesses. How large a world is it? Suppose we count as a big business any corporation with assets worth more than $250 million. There are roughly three thousand such businesses in America. Over half of them are in finance, mainly insurance and banking. About one fifth are in manufacturing. The rest are to be found in transportation, utilities, communication, trade. Just to get an idea of scale, the "richest" enterprise in the nation in 1996 was probably Citicorp, with assets of $257 billion.

The largest *industrial* firm was Ford, with assets of over $243 billion. *These two firms together probably commanded as much wealth (assets) as all the thirteen million proprietorships of the nation.* The firms change from time to time—GM and IBM have both had mighty falls—but the size pattern remains.* The top five hundred firms—fewer than one tenth of one percent of the total number—account for roughly 75 percent of all sales. *Indeed, if we take only the biggest one hundred firms, we find that they are the source of almost half the sales of the entire industrial sector.*

A PARADE OF BUSINESS FIRMS

We shall have a good deal to investigate in later chapters about the world of big business. But it might be useful to end this initial survey with a dramatization of the problem. The figures depict the statistics of a few years back, but the visual impression is still there.

Suppose we lined up our roughly 21 million businesses in order of size, starting with the smallest, along an imaginary road from San Francisco to New York. There will be 5,500 businesses to the mile, or about one per foot. Suppose further that we planted a flag

---

*There is no official designation of a "big" business. We have used the *Fortune* magazine list of the top 500 industrial firms, plus their list of the top 50 firms in banking, insurance, finance, transportation, utilities, and retailing. Rule of thumb: To make it into the Fortune 500 in the 1990s, you need around $500 million in sales or about $100 million in assets.

for each business. The height of the flagpole represents the volume of sales: each $10,000 in sales is shown by one foot of pole.

The line of flagpoles is a very interesting sight. From San Francisco to about Reno, Nevada, it is almost unnoticeable, a row of poles only a few feet high. From Reno eastward the poles increase in height until, near Columbus, Ohio—about four fifths of the way across the nation—flags fly about 10 feet in the air, symbolizing $100,000 in sales. Looking backward from Columbus, we can see almost two thirds of all firms have sales of less than that amount.

But as we approach the eastern terminus, the poles suddenly begin to mount. There are about one million firms in the country with sales over $500,000. These corporations occupy the last 75 miles of the 3,000-mile road. There are 700,000 firms with sales of over $1 million. They occupy the last 50 miles of the road, with poles at least 100 feet high. Then there are 2,300 firms with sales of $50,000,000 or more. They take up the last quarter mile before the city limits, flags flying at cloud heights, 5,000 feet up.

But this is not the climax. At the very gates of New York, on the last 100 feet of the last mile, we find the 100 largest industrial firms. They have sales of at least $5 billion, so that their flags are already miles high, above the clouds. Along the last 10 feet of the road, there are the ten largest companies. Their sales are roughly $40 billion and up: Their flags fly literally in the sky.

As we said, the figures refer to dollar values a few years earlier. The flags would all fly about twice as high today—two feet off the ground from San Francisco to Reno; stratospheric in New York. But the flagpole parade would look about the same.

BIGNESS IN WORLD PERSPECTIVE

Finally—and a very important finally—we have to put the American picture into a world context. Capitalism everywhere is big business capitalism. Moreover, the size of firms has been growing more rapidly in Europe and Japan than here, so that U.S. firms are actually smaller than they used to be, compared to world GDP and to their foreign competitors. Among the fifty largest firms in the world, ranked by sales, seventeen are American, two are Japanese, six are German, and two are British. None of the twenty biggest banks are American!

HOUSEHOLDS AND INCOMES

The two worlds of business give us a sense of the economic structure of things. But there is obviously more than business firms in the economy. Another major element in the landscape is households—the sixty-nine million families and twenty-nine million single-dwelling individuals or nonfamily households who were the people in the economic picture in the mid 1990s.

What is it about households that interests economists? One thing is that households are the source of our labor force, a matter we'll be looking into later. But more striking in this first survey of the economy is that households give us an overview of the distribution of income in the economy. Looking at the panorama of the nation's families and single dwellers gives us an essential picture of its riches and poverty. Important note: These numbers do not reflect the dynamics of income distribution mentioned in our introduction. We will come to that problem in due course. What we need, to begin with, however, is a general impression of the extent and magnitude of poverty. That changes only gradually, despite its unhealthy growth in recent years.

There are many ways of describing income distribution. We will use a method that will divide the country into five equal layers, like a great cake. The layers will help us give dollars-and-cents definitions of what we usually have in mind when we speak of the poor, the working class, the middle class, and so on. As we will see, the amounts are not at all what most of us imagine.

We begin with the bottom layer, the poor. By our definition, this will include all the households in the bottom 20 percent of the nation. From data gathered by the Census Bureau, we know that the highest income of a family in this bottom slice of the five-layered cake was under $17,000 in 1995. For purposes of comparison, the level of income designated by the Department of Commerce as "near-poverty" for a four-person family was $16,000 for that year. Thus we exaggerate, but not too much, in thinking of the bottom fifth of the nation as mainly poor, or near-poor.

The box headed "Poverty" on page 50 shows some of the characteristics of poor families, but there are two additional facts about poverty that we should note. First, not all families who are counted as poor in any given census remain poor in the next census. About one seventh of all poor households are young people just starting their careers. Some of these low-income beginners will escape from poverty. In addition, about a third of the members of the poverty class are older people. Many of these were not poor in an earlier, more productive stage of their economic lives. At the same time, this also means that some families that are not poor when a census is taken will fall into poverty at a later stage of their lives. The moral of this is that poverty is not entirely static. At any moment, some families are escaping from poverty, some entering it. What counts, of course, is whether the net movement is in or out. As we will see in our next chapter, it has recently been slowly in.

A second characteristic also deserves to be noted. Three-quarters of the families below the poverty line have at least one wage earner in the labor force. Thus their poverty reflects inadequate earnings. A considerable amount of poverty, in other words, reflects the fact that some jobs do not pay enough to lift a jobholder above the low-income level. In some regions, certain jobs are so low-paying that even two jobholders in a family (especially if one works only seasonally) will not suffice to bring the family out of poverty. This is often the case, for example, with migrant farm workers, or with immigrants who must seek employment in the least desirable jobs.

We usually define the working class in terms of certain occupations. We call a factory worker—but not a salesclerk—working class, even though the factory employee may make more than a salesclerk.

For our purposes, however, we will just take the next two layers of the income cake and call them working class. This will include the 40 percent of the population that is above the poor. We choose this method to find out how large an income a family can make and still remain in the working class, as we have defined it. The answer is up to $40,000. To put it differently, 40 percent of the families in the country in the mid 1990s earned between $17,000 and $40,000 a year.

With the bottom three fifths of the nation tagged—roughly one fifth poor, two fifths working class—we are ready to look into the income levels of upper echelons. First, the rich. Where do riches begin? The realistic answer does not deal with incomes, but with wealth—the assets people own, whether in stocks and bonds, real estate, or whatever. We'll come to that shortly.

POVERTY

In the mid 1990s, thirty-six million Americans lived below income levels officially designated as "poverty." What characteristics distinguished these families? Here are some:

Old Age: A little over 10 percent were retirees.

Youth: A poor household was more likely to be headed by someone under 25 than by a person aged 25–64.

Color: About 30 percent of poor persons were black. About one third of black families and half of all black children were poor.

Sex: A poor family was six times as likely to be headed by a female as a male.

Schooling: The heads of almost half of all poor families had not graduated from high school.

Of course many characteristics overlap and reinforce one another: Poor families are often old, black, and uneducated. No one characteristic is decisive in "making" a family poor. For instance, families are poor not just because they have no schooling, but they have no schooling because they are poor. Poverty breeds poverty.

Under the rich are a considerably larger group that we will call the upper class. We shall count the upper 5 percent of the nation in this class. It comprises such occupations as successful doctors and lawyers and businessmen, top airline pilots, upper-middle management, even a few professors. How much income does it take to get into the top 5 percent? In 1995 the boundary line was crossed at $123,000.

This leaves us with the middle class—the class to which we all think we belong. By our method of cutting the cake, the middle class includes 35 percent of the nation—everyone between the $40,000 working-class top income and the $123,000 upper-class lowest income. In 1995 an average white married couple, both working, earned a little over $39,000—almost enough to enter middle-class economic territory. No

DISTRIBUTION OF FAMILIES BY NET WORTH, 1988*

Percentage of families	Net worth
Lowest 25 percent	Less than $5,000
Next 30 percent	$5,000 to $50,000
Next 35 percent	$50,000 to $250,000
Top 10 percent	Over $250,000

* Note that these figures—the most up-to-date we have—are not nearly so recent as those on income distribution. It simply takes longer to gather the data on wealth. For the most authoritative study, see Edward N. Wolff, *Top Heavy* (New York: 20th Century Fund, 1996).

wonder a middle-class feeling pervades American society, regardless of the occupation or social milieu from which families come.†

It is obvious that there are great extremes of income distribution in the United States. Some years ago Paul Samuelson, perhaps the nation's most famous economist, made the observation that if we built an income pyramid out of children's blocks, with each layer representing $1,000 of income, the peak would be far higher than the Eiffel Tower, but most of us would be within a yard of the ground.

Even more striking than the inequality of income, however, is the inequality of wealth, illustrated in the table above.

As we can see, a fourth of all households had virtually no wealth at all. This obviously includes the lowest fifth ("the poor") and the lower portion of the group we have designated the working class. The next 30 percent have modest assets—largely comprising the net value of their homes, cars, savings accounts, etc. This takes us through the layers of working-class families, to the doorstep of the middle class. Here assets begin to amount to something, and by the time we have reached the threshold of the upper class, a typical household measures its net worth at a quarter of a million dollars—a substantial home, some insurance, and other savings. Here is where stocks and bonds also enter: about 20 percent of Americans own securities.

Recent figures tell us something additional about the distribution of wealth at the very top. In 1988 there were 940,000 families with a net

†Maybe you wonder how an "average white married couple" could enter an income group that we have defined as being not average. The answer is that not every household in our national layer cake was white or married with both husband and wife working. For a look at the numbers, see the *Statistical Abstract 1994,* Tables 71a and 71b.

worth of $1 million or more—about 2 percent of all families. These assets included the value of the homes or private business enterprises owned by these families. If we count up only the families with $1 million or more in financial assets, such as stocks and bonds and insurance, the number falls sharply to about 250,000 families—one half of 1 percent of all family units. By the 1990s, this figure was perhaps double that.

How much wealth do millionaires own in all? We are not sure. Estimates for the 1960s indicated that millionaire families owned half to three quarters of the value of all stocks and bonds and private real estate. These figures can change as inflation waxes and wanes or as the stock market fluctuates. All during the late 1960s and 1970s, as inflation was gathering momentum, the level of stock prices was virtually unchanged. As a result, a family with an average portfolio of stocks suffered a very substantial loss of its real wealth during these years. Indeed, a person with a $1 million portfolio in 1972 would have lost half his or her purchasing power by 1981. Starting that year, however, stocks began to rise, and in 1985 and 1986 we saw a boom in which stock prices doubled, followed by another boom that doubled them again by 1992. As to what happened thereafter, we'll have to wait until we reach chapter 18.

A PARADE OF INCOMES

Suppose that like our parade of flags across the nation representing the sales of business firms, we lined up the population in order of its income. Assume the height of the middle household to be 6 feet, representing a median income of $34,000 in 1995. This will be our height, as observers. What would our parade look like?*

It would begin with a few families *below* the ground, for there are some households with negative incomes; that is, they report losses for the year. Mainly these are families with business losses, and their negative incomes are not matched by general poverty. Following close on their heels comes a long line of dwarfs who make up about one fifth of all families, people less than three feet tall. Some are shorter than one foot.

Only after the parade is half over do we reach people whose faces are at our level. Then come the giants. When we reach the last 5 percent of the parade—incomes above $100,000—people are 20 feet tall. At the end of the parade, people tower 600 to 6,000 feet into the air—one hundred to one thousand times as tall as the middle height. What is the largest income in the country? We do not know: Probably our sixty-odd billionaires have incomes of over $100 million.

---

* Adapted from the brilliant description of an "income parade" in Jan Pen, *Income Distribution,* trans. Trevor S. Preston (New York: Praeger, 1971), pp. 48–59.

GOVERNMENT

We have almost completed our first overview of the economy, but there remains one last institution with which we must again in acquaintance: the government. How shall we size up so vast and complex an organization? There is no simple or single way. Only as we proceed along will the government sector come into clearer focus. Just the same, we have to begin somewhere. These figures will start us off:

PUBLIC AND PRIVATE SECTORS, 1996 EST.

	Public	Private
Total output ($ billion)	87.5	6,701.0
Total employees (million)	19.2	107.5

The figures show that, measured in ordinary economic terms, by the size of income or the number of employees, the private sector is much larger than the public. But clearly that understates the size and wealth of government. What dollar figure should we put on the nation's land, one third of which is owned by the federal government? What is the economic value of the national defense establishment? What is the value of the government's exclusive right to print money? When we begin to ask such questions, the idea of comparing the relative sizes of business and government falls apart.

Nevertheless, there are two points worth making strongly as we try to take an initial reading on the place of government within the economy. The first is that "government" does not just mean the federal government. As we shall see, the federal government has a crucial role to play in the economy at many levels. But we should not lose sight of the fact that state and local governments are much more important than the federal government as a source of employment—roughly four to five times as many people work for states and counties and cities as for Washington.

In addition, state and local governments produce much more public output than does the federal government in many important areas. Public output is part of total output. If we take away defense as a special case, state and local government is therefore a much larger contributor to public output than is the federal government.* The table following is worth looking at from that point of view, for it reminds us of the range of nonfederal activities that "government" includes, a range much wider than the bureaucratic paper-pushing the word often evokes.

Second, the variety of public outputs reminds us that government is not just a dead weight on the economy, as so many tend to think. Anyone who has ever gone to a public school, been treated in a public hospital, traveled on a public road, or flown in a plane guided by a public beacon system has been the recipient of government production and knows how vital public output can be. Even those who emphasize the maddening bureaucracy and the inefficiency that can come from government activity (although government has no monopoly on either) should reflect that the system of private enterprise itself depends on the invisible output of law enforcement on which this economy, like all economies, rests.

FEDERAL VERSUS STATE AND LOCAL EXPENDITURES, 1995

	Federal $ billion	State and Local $ billion
National defense	291	0
Education	50	343
Highways	35	68
Health	99	32
Housing & utilities	13	19
Natural resources	49	13

*Welfare expenditures are not part of public output. These originate mainly with the federal government. This makes Washington a bigger *spender* than the states and localities, but not a bigger *producer.* More on this when we turn to a consideration of how output is counted in the chapters ahead.

FOUR

The Trend of Things

We begin with a look back and a look ahead. In our introduction we stressed the importance of troubling new problems that form the very reason for being of this new edition of our text. If we were reading this text for the first time, we would be expecting those new problems to show up in these first chapters. But we are not quite ready to consider them. The reason is that we need perspective to consider what lies not too far ahead, just as a doctor needs to know his patient's history before pronouncing a diagnosis or writing out a prescription.

Hence we turn to the "trend of things" to get a feel for an aspect of economics we have not yet studied—not a "map" of our economy, but a feeling for its life story. There is no doubt as to what that first impression will be. It is a sense of growth. Everything has been getting larger. Business firms have been growing in size; labor unions are bigger; there are more households and each household is richer; government is much larger. And underlying all this, the extent of the market system itself—the great circular flow of transactions—has been steadily increasing in size.

Growth is not, of course, the only thing we notice. Businesses are different as well as bigger when we compare the early 1900s with today. There are far more corporations now than in the old days, far more diversified businesses, fewer family firms. Households are different because almost half of all married women work away from home. Labor unions are no longer mainly craft unions, limited by one occupation. Government is not only bigger, but has a different philosophy.

ECONOMIC GROWTH

Nevertheless, it is growth that first commands our attention. The camera vision of the economy gives us a picture that requires an ever-larger screen. The screen has to widen because it must encompass an ever-widening river of output. Hence the first thing we must do is examine this phenomenal rise in the dollar value of total output, represented in the following graph. We call this value of output, which includes all the goods and services produced by the public sector as well as those produced by the private sector, our *gross domestic product,* abbreviated as GDP. In our next chapter we will define GDP more carefully. Here we want to talk about its startling rise from 1900 to 1997. We will examine the years after 1980 in our next part.

As we can see, the dollar value of all output over that earlier span

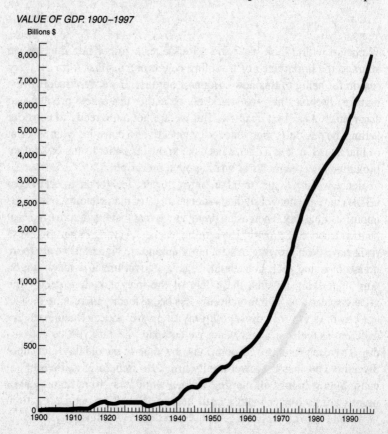

VALUE OF GDP. 1900–1997

Billions $

rose by a factor of about one hundred. But undoubtedly a cautionary thought has already crossed your mind. If we measure the growth of output by comparing the dollar value of production over time, what seems to be a growth in actual economic activity may be no more than a rise in prices.

That cautionary thought is absolutely right. Suppose an economy produces only wheat, and suppose that wheat sold for a dollar in 1900 and four dollars in 1980. Now imagine that the actual output of wheat is unchanged, one million tons in both years. If we compute the GDP for 1900 we get $1 million (a million tons at one dollar each), but if we compute the GDP for 1980, it is $4 million! So we have to wring the inflation out of these figures. The way we do so is to use *the same prices* in computing the value of output in both years. Obviously, whatever price we use in our example, GDP will not rise.

If we calculate the value of GDP by using the different prices of the years in which the output was produced, we call the dollar total *current* or *nominal* GDP. But if we compute the values of GDP over several years, using the price of *only one year,* we call the result *real* GDP. It is real in the sense that we have pretty well eliminated the change in the value of output that is just the result of higher or lower prices, so that our results measure actual changes in production, not just changes in selling prices.

In the chart on page 58 we show what happens to the upward swooping curve of nominal GDP from 1900 to 1996, when we use the prices of a single year—in this case 1972—to calculate the value of output (GDP) in each and every year. The result is still impressive—a rise of about tenfold. But clearly this is much less dramatic than the rise before we adjusted for inflation.

There remains a last adjustment to be made. Not only has output increased, but so also has population. In 1900, United States population was 76 million; in 1996 it was about 267 million. To bring our real GDP down to life-size, we have to divide it by population to get GDP per person or per capita. When we do so, we get a quite astonishing result. Looking back not just to the early 1900s, but as far as we can piece together statistics, we find that the pace of real per capita growth has been amazingly steady. There are swings up and down, some of them serious. But most of the swings are within 10 percent of a main trend line.

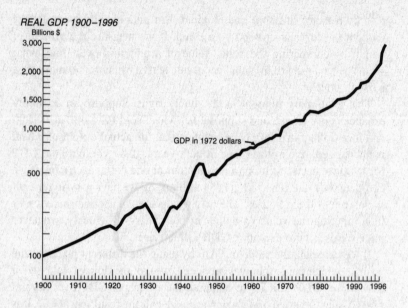

REAL GDP. 1900–1996
Billions $

GDP in 1972 dollars

The trend itself comes to about 1.5 percent a year in real terms per capita. Although 1.5 percent a year may not sound like much, this figure allows us to double our real per capita living standards every forty-seven years. This is Adam Smith's growth model come to life!

How do we explain this long, steady upward trend? Essentially there are two reasons. First, the *quantity* of inputs going into the economic process increased. In 1900 our labor force was 27 million. In 1980 it was 108 million. Obviously, larger inputs of labor produce larger outputs of goods and services. Our quantity of capital inputs increased as well. For instance, in 1900 the total horsepower energy delivered by "prime movers"—engines of all kinds, work animals, ships, trains, and so forth—was 65 million horsepower. In 1980 it was almost 30 *billion.*

Second, the *quality* of inputs improved. The population working in 1980 was not only more numerous than in 1900, it was better trained and better schooled. One overall gauge of this is the amount of education stored up in the work force. In 1900, when only 6.4 percent of the working population had gone beyond grade school, there were 223 million man-years of schooling embodied in the population. In 1980, when two thirds of the population had finished high school, the stock of education embodied in the population had grown to over a billion man-years.

The quality of capital has also increased, along with its quantity. As an indication of the importance of the changing quality of capital, consider the contribution made to our output by the availability of surfaced roads. In 1900 there were about 150,000 miles of such roads. In 1980 there were almost 4 million miles. That is an increase of over twenty-five times. But that increase does not begin to measure the difference in the transport capability of the two road systems, one of them graveled, narrow, built for traffic that averaged 10 to 20 miles per hour; the other concrete or asphalt, multilane, fast-paced.

There are still other sources of growth, such as shifts in occupations and efficiencies of large-scale operation, but the main ones are the increase in the quantity and quality of inputs. Of the two, *improvements in the quality of inputs—in human skills, in improved designs of capital equipment—have been far more important than mere increases in quantity.* Better skills and technology enable the labor force to increase its productivity, the amount of goods and services it can turn out in a given time.

THE TREND TO BIG BUSINESS

Now let us turn to business. Here one change immediately strikes the eye. There is a marked decline of the independent, small business—with its self-employed worker—as a main form of enterprise.

In 1900 there were about 8 million independent enterprises, including 5.7 million farms. By the early 1990s, as we saw in our last chapter, the number of proprietorships had grown to over 14 million, including 2.1 million farms. Meanwhile, the labor force itself more than tripled. Thus *as a percentage of all persons working, the proportion of self-employed has fallen from about 30 percent in 1900 to around 9 percent today.*

With the decline of the self-employed worker has come the rise of the giant firm. Back in 1900 the giant corporation was just arriving on the scene. In 1901 financier J. P. Morgan created the first billion-dollar company when he formed the United States Steel Corporation out of a dozen smaller enterprises. In that year the total capitalization of all corporations valued at more than $1 million was $5 billion. By 1904 it was $20 billion. In 1985 it was about $10 *trillion*.

It hardly comes as a surprise that the main trend of the past eighty years has been the emergence of big business. More interesting is the question of whether big business is continuing to grow. This is a more difficult question to answer, for it depends on what we mean by growth.

Certainly the place of the biggest companies within the world of corporations has been rising, as our next table shows. Marx was right in predicting this trend.

LARGEST MANUFACTURERS' SHARE OF ASSETS (%)

	1948	1960	1970	1975	1983	1991 (est.)*
100 largest corporations	40.2	46.4	48.5	45.0	48.3	69.5
200 largest corporations	48.2	56.3	60.4	57.5	60.8	88.7

* Latest available figures.

We can see that the top one hundred companies held approximately half again as large a share of total corporate wealth in the 1980s and early 1990s as did the top *two hundred* companies in 1948. This growing concentration of assets in the hands of the mightiest companies is not the same thing, however, as an increase in monopolization, as we usually define that term. Monopolization refers to the share of a company within a given market, such as GM's share of the auto industry. Within the preponderance of markets in the economy, the shares of giant firms has *not* markedly risen, and has often fallen, even though the total wealth of the corporate world has been steadily drifting into their hands.

Can we explain the long-term trend downward the concentration of business assets, as we did the trend toward growth in GDP? By and large, economists would stress three main reasons for the appearance of giant enterprise. The first reason is that advances in technology have made possible the mass production of goods or services at falling costs. The rise of bigness in business is very much a result of technology. Without the steam engine, the lathe, the railroad, it is difficult to imagine how big business would have emerged in the first place.

But technology went on to do more than make large-scale production possible. Typically it also brought an economic effect that we call *economies of scale.* That is, technology not only enlarged, it also cheapened the process of production. Costs per unit fell as output rose.

The process is perfectly exemplified in the huge reduction of cost in producing automobiles on an assembly line rather than one car at a time (see box below).

Economies of scale provided further powerful impetus toward a growth in size. The firm that pioneered in the introduction of mass-production technology usually secured a competitive selling advantage over its competitors, enabling it to grow in size and thereby to increase its advantage still further. These cost-reducing advantages were important causes of the initial emergence of giant companies in many industries. Similarly, the absence of such technologies explains why corporate giants did not emerge in all fields.

FROM PIN FACTORY TO ASSEMBLY LINE

We recall Adam Smith's pin factory (Chapter Two). Here is a later version of that division of labor, in the early Ford assembly lines:

"Just how were the main assembly lines and lines of component production and supply kept in harmony? For the chassis alone, from 1,000 to 4,000 pieces of each component had to be furnished each day at just the right point and right minute: a single failure, and the whole mechanism would come to a jarring standstill. . . . Superintendents had to know every hour just how many components were being produced and how many were in stock. Whenever danger of shortage appeared, the shortage chaser—a familiar figure in all automobile factories—flung himself into the breach. Counters and checkers reported to him. Verifying in person any ominous news, he mobilized the foreman concerned to repair deficiencies. Three times a day he made typed reports in manifold to the factory clearinghouse, at the same time chalking on blackboards in the clearinghouse office a statement of results in each factory-production department and each assembling department."*

Such systematizing in itself resulted in astonishing increases in productivity. With each operation analyzed and subdivided into its simplest components, with a steady stream of work passing before stationary men, with a relentless but manageable pace of work, the total time required to assemble a car dropped astonishingly. Within a single year, the time required to assemble a motor fell from 10 hours to 3 hours 46 minutes: to build a chassis, from 12 hours and 28 minutes to 1 hour and 33 minutes. A stopwatch man was told to observe a 3-minute assembly in which men assembled rods and pistons, a simple operation. The job was divided into three jobs, and half the men turned out the same output as before.

---

* Allan Nevins, *Ford, the Times, the Man, the Company* (New York: Scribner's, 1954), p. 1,507.

Second, business concentration is also a result of a corporate mergers. Ever since J. P. Morgan assembled U.S. Steel, mergers have been a major source of corporate growth. At the very end of the nineteenth century there was the first great merger wave, out of which came the first huge companies, including U.S. Steel. In 1890 most industries were competitive, without a single company dominating the field. By 1904 one or two giant firms, usually created by mergers, had arisen to control at least half the output in seventy-eight different industries.

Again, between 1951 and 1960 one fifth of the top one thousand corporations disappeared—not because they failed, but because they were bought up by other corporations. In all, mergers have accounted for about two fifths of the increase in concentration between 1950 and 1970; internal growth accounts for the rest.

Finally, concentration is accelerated by the business cycle. Depressions or recessions plunge many smaller firms into bankruptcy and make it possible for larger, more financially secure firms to buy them up very cheaply. This is once more as Marx anticipated. When industries are threatened, the weak producers go under; the stronger ones emerge relatively stronger than before. Consider, for example, that three once-prominent American automobile producers—Studebaker, Packard, and Kaiser Motors—succumbed to the mild recessions of the 1950s and 1960s, and to the pressure of foreign competition. In 1980 Chrysler skirted bankruptcy.

MERGER MANIA

Has the trend to bigness leveled off? A few years ago it seemed that the trend was winding down. But the 1980s witnessed another vast merger wave—indeed, the largest such wave in history. In 1984 some three thousand giant mergers took place, involving $124 billion in assets. In

1985 the total was even higher. In that year there were at least five mergers, *each of which was larger than the total value of all the mergers of the premerger decade.* Just as examples, General Electric bought RCA for $6.3 billion; Philip Morris bought General Foods for $5.8 billion; and General Motors bought Hughes Aircraft for $5.1 billion. The trend continued through 1989, when another four thousand-odd mergers amounted in themselves to $254 billion.

SIGNS OF CHANGE

Only a few years ago, when the previous edition of this book went to press, we left matters more or less at this point: there had certainly been an extraordinary wave of amalgamation, but there were some signs that the wave was coming to an end. Indeed a new phenomenon of "downsizing" had appeared on the scene, and we wrote:

> One after another, giant firms that appeared to be unassailable because of their very size have turned out to be economic dinosaurs, unable to hold their own in the high-tech, quick-turnaround, just-in-time production patterns of the mid-1990s. General Motors, International Business Machines, Sears Roebuck have all started on major downsizings, trying to regain a capacity for flexibility and efficiency that they lost as a consequence of growth for growth's sake alone.

Where are we today with respect to this important question? The answer is that we are in a period of considerable uncertainty, as a phenomenon that had only begun to loom large in the early 1990s appears larger and more upsetting each year. This is the new technological/organizational reorganization of business that we call globalization. This new word in our economic vocabulary refers to a change of such importance that we will devote a whole chapter to it at the end of this book.

Meanwhile—now that we have tipped our readers off and hopefully whetted your appetites—we are going to finish the task we set for ourselves in this chapter. We have a first impression of the trend of business growth, but there remain two other sectors that require a similar introduction—labor and government.

As you will see, they too pose problems of great importance that require our attention later in this book. All the more reason then to do our homework on their not-so-distant pasts.

THE ROLLER COASTER IN LABOR

In their formative years, labor unions grew in strength roughly as a counterpart to the growth of big business. Unions were, after all, largely a social response to the pressures exerted by massive enterprises on their work forces. Thus the numbers of men and women in unions increased from less than a half million in 1897 to just over 3.5 million in 1929. Thereafter membership remained static until the passage of the National Labor Relations Act of 1935, which legitimized industrial as well as craft unionization. That green light soon doubled union membership, and this number grew still further in the postwar years, until by the mid-1950s some 18 million workers—31 percent of the labor force—belonged to either a craft or an industrial labor organization.

There has been a dramatic decline since then, as the percentage of unionized labor in the national labor force has been cut in half. What lies behind this extraordinary fall? There is more than one answer. The decline begins with the swelling of employment in the service sector during the 1950s and 1960s—a sector populated by small businesses and a heavy preponderance of female workers, both relatively difficult to unionize. At the same time, the decline reflects a growing inertia on the part of the top labor leadership in the 1960s, content with its comfortable bargains with management. The decline gains further momentum in the 1970s when management turns more aggressively against unions, under the duress of shrinking profit margins. Finally, government completes the decline during the Reagan years with an increasingly open antiunion stance.

Perhaps more significant than this roller-coaster profile of labor union strength is the failure of the United States to accord a legitimacy to unions comparable to that found in Canada and in virtually all European nations. There has been nothing like the decline of union strength abroad that we have seen here, and the strongly adversarial position of both government and management toward unions in our country has to be compared with very different attitudes abroad. In Germany, for example, union leaders sit on large corporation boards by law. If this labor-management accord works, as it is supposed to, both to moderate inflationary wage demands and to enhance managerial efficiency, it will give our European competitors a substantial competitive edge. For the moment, however, such a way of dealing with the "labor problem" does not seem to be within the American imagination. As we promised, we will come back to this very important issue later on.

BIG GOVERNMENT EMERGES

We pass now to the last great trend of the economy, a trend whose end result has been the emergence of that large government apparatus we noted in our previous chapter.

There are three quite different ways of measuring the rise of the public sector. The first is to examine the proportion of GDP that government directly produces or purchases. This might be regarded as a rough indication of the degree to which we have become a nationalized economy.

A second way is to inquire into the extent to which the government reallocates incomes by taxing some persons and giving others *transfer payments* such as Social Security benefits or welfare or unemployment insurance. This might be regarded as an index of the degree to which we have become a welfare state.

Last is the extent to which government interferes in the working of the economy by regulating various aspects of economic life or by exercising its economic powers in other ways. By far the most difficult to measure exactly, this might be thought of as an indication of the extent to which we have moved in the direction of a guided or controlled capitalism.

No one will be surprised to learn that all three indicators are up over the long run. Take the trend of direct government production or purchases. In 1929 government bought less than 10 percent of total output; in 1980 it bought about 20 percent. Most of this increase, it ought to be noted, comes from two sources: a very large rise in federal spending for defense and a very substantial growth of state and local spending on education and roads. Defense aside, the federal government is not a big buyer of goods and services, impressions to the contrary notwithstanding. Moreover, the percentage of federal government buying of GDP has been stable for twenty-five years.

But certainly the federal government is a big spender of money. This brings us to the second indication of the growth of government, its welfare function. Back in 1929 less than 1 percent of GDP was redistributed as a transfer payment by government. In 1980 transfer payments amounted to roughly 11 percent of GDP. The bulk of this was federal expenditures for Social Security, Medicare, and other "safety net" purposes. It is the growth in government transfers, not the growth in government purchasing, that accounts for the real bulge in public spending. The two combined streams come to about one third of GDP. Here we only want to call attention to the fact that this has been a worldwide trend, and that most European capitalisms spend or transfer a considerably larger fraction of their GDPs through government hands than we do.

Last, there is the third measure of government size—the extent of its intervention, the bulk of its sheer presence as a supervisor or regulator of the system.

Because of its varied nature, and because the importance of government intervention is not always shown by the amount of money that an agency spends or the number of personnel it employs, this is a trend that defies easy measurement. Much of the spending that we have noted, for example, is carried out through established departments of the executive branch of government, especially Health and Welfare, from which Social Security checks flow, and the Defense Department, source of military spending.

But we ought to have at least some indication, however impressionistic and incomplete, of the widening reach of government concern within various areas of the economic system. The following list gives us some inkling of the variety and importance of these functions:

Environmental Protection Agency *administers antipollution legislation*
Federal Reserve Board *regulates banks*
Federal Communications Commission *assigns airwave frequencies to stations*
Federal Trade Commission *polices business activities in restraint of trade*
Interstate Commerce Commission *regulates rail, canal, and truck industry*
National Labor Relations Board *supervises union elections*
National Science Foundation *supports scientific research*
Tariff Commission *holds hearings on tariff matters*

Some agencies, such as the Tariff Commission, are almost a hundred years old. Others, like the Environmental Protection Agency, are relatively new. But obviously the range and reach of government intervention into the economy has increased enormously, whether we look back a century or only a relatively short time. Perhaps in the future that long trend may come to a halt or may even be permanently reversed. That is a matter to be considered as we go along. But first we must seek to understand the reasons for the long-run upward trend in all indicators: government buying, government transfers, government intervention.

There is, of course, no simple or even irrefutable answer. But a backward glance over history suggests these causes:

The growing size of business itself has evoked a need for government intervention. As business firms have increased in size, private decisions have become fraught with social consequences. The decisions of big business have widespread repercussions. Building or not building a plant may spell prosperity or decline for a town, even a state. Cutthroat competition can spell ruin for an industry. Polluting a river can ruin a region. Much government effort, at the local and state as well as federal levels, represents attempts to prevent big business from creating social or economic problems, or to cope with problems it has created.

Technology has brought a need for public supervision. An impressive amount of government effort goes into the regulation of problem-creating technologies. Examples: the network of state and local highway and police authorities that deal with the automobile; the panoply of agencies designed to cope with airplanes, television and radio, atomic energy, new drugs, and weaponry. As long as technology increases its power to affect our social and natural environment, it is likely that public supervision will also increase.

Urbanization has created a need for centralized administration. City life has its appeals, but it also has it perils. Men and women cannot live in crowded quarters without police, public health, traffic, sanitation, and educational facilities far more complex than those needed in a rural setting. Government is, and always has been, concentrated in cities. As a nation urbanizes, it requires more government.

Unification of the economy has given us additional problems. Industrialization knits an economy together into a kind of vast, interlocked machinery. An unindustrialized, localized economy is like a pile of sand: if you poke a finger into one side of it, some businesses and individuals will be affected, but those on the other side of the pile will remain undisturbed. The growing scale and specialization of industrial operations unify the sandpile. You poke one side of it, and the entire pile shakes. Problems can no longer be localized. The difficulties of the economy grow in extent: there is a need for a national, not a local, en-

ergy program, for national transportation, urban, and educational programs. Government—largely federal government—is the principal
means by which such problems are handled.

   Economic malfunction has brought public intervention. Fifty or
seventy-five years ago the prevailing attitude toward the economy was
a kind of awed respect. People felt that the economy was best left
alone, that it was fruitless as well as ill-advised to try to change its normal workings. That attitude changed once and for all with the advent of
the Great Depression. In the ensuing collapse, the role of government
was enlarged greatly, to restore the economy to working order. The
trauma of the Depression and the determination to prevent its recur-
rence were a watershed in the trend of government spending and government intervention. Keynes's thinking played a very important part
in this transition to a mixed economy, and not even the most conservative government today has any intention of returning to a pure
laissez-faire system. That is no longer possible.

   *Last, but not least, we no longer live in a society in which old-age re-
tirement, medical expenses, and income during periods of unemployment are felt to be properly the responsibility of the individuals
concerned.* For better or worse, these and similar responsibilities have
been gradually assumed by governments in all capitalist nations. In
fact, the United States is a laggard in these matters compared with
many European capitalist states. Here lie crucial reasons for the
swelling volume of state, local, and federal production and purchase
that have steadily enlarged the place of government within the
economy.*

   No doubt there are other causes that could be added to this list. Bureaucracies have ways of feeding on themselves. Deficits have swollen
government spending, for reasons, and with consequences, that we will
look into later. But the overall conclusion is already evident. In modern
capitalism, government is a major factor in the economic system. More
and more, we *make* our history, rather than just waiting for it to happen.
How well government fulfills this function, and to what extent it real-
izes the hopes that have been thrust upon it, are themes that will constantly occupy us as we continue along.

---

*For an excellent account of the successes, failures, and needs that surround government
intervention into markets, see Robert Kuttner, *Everything for Sale* (New York: Alfred A.
Knopf, 1997).

II

MACROECONOMICS— THE ANALYSIS OF PROSPERITY AND RECESSION

FIVE

The GDP

One of the reasons for the mystification that obscures economics is the vocabulary it employs. Not only does it use common, ordinary words, such as *saving* or *investing,* in ways that are not exactly the way we use them in everyday talk, but it leans on barbarous and intimidating terms like *macroeconomics* or *gross domestic product.*

It would be nice if we could purge economics of its jargon, but that would be like asking doctors to tell us about our troubles in plain English. Instead, we must learn to speak a certain amount of economics—that is, to become familiar with, and easy about, some of the basic terms in which economists tell about our economic condition.

One of these is that odd word "macroeconomics." It comes from the Greek *macro,* meaning big, and the implication is that macroeconomics therefore grapples with very big problems. It does, including such problems as inflation and recession and unemployment and economic growth. But that is not what distinguishes macro from its brother, "microeconomics," whom we will meet later. Rather, macroeconomics refers to a perspective, a vantage point, that throws into high relief certain aspects of the economic system.

What does the economy look like from the macro perspective? The view is not unlike that which we have gained in the chapters just past. We look down on the economy, as from a plane, to see it as a vast landscape populated by business firms, households, government agencies. Later, when we take up the micro perspective, we will examine the selfsame landscape from a worm's-eye rather than a bird's-eye view, with surprising consequences as to the features of the landscape that spring into sharp focus.

The purpose of looking down on the economy from the macro vantage point is that it allows us to see, more clearly than from ground level, a process of crucial and central importance. This is the ceaseless activity of production on a national scale, the never-ending creation and re-creation of the wealth by which the country replenishes and renews and expands its material life. This great central flow, on which we all depend, is called the *gross domestic product,* often abbreviated as GDP. When TV newscasters say that GDP has gone up or down, what they mean is that the river of output has gotten larger or smaller, that we are producing more or less. Learning about why production varies is the first task of macroeconomics.

WHAT GDP IS MADE OF

We start to unravel the question by looking more closely at the river itself. One thing is immediately clear. The flow of output arises from the cooperation of the factors of production—from the efforts of the labor force mustered from the nation's households, working with capital and land mainly owned by the nation's businesses, under the rules and laws established by the government. We can literally see the flow of production originating in the 10 million farms and factories, offices and agencies, over which we fly. It is from these wellsprings that the river of national output is formed.

As we look down on it, the river seems at first to be made up of an unclassifiable collection of outputs. There are hundreds of thousands, perhaps millions, of kinds of goods and services in the stream of production—foods of every conceivable kind, spectrums of clothing, catalogs of machinery, jumbles of junk. But at second look, we can see that this vast and variegated output can be divided into two basic sorts of production. One of them consists of goods and services that will usually be bought by private households, though also by government employees for individual use: cars, haircuts, jewelry, meat, health care, weather forecasts. We call this branch of the river of production *consumption,* and the various goods and services in it *consumers' goods.*

The consumption branch of our production process is familiar to us. But looking again from our macro vantage point, we can see that there are also goods and services that *never end up in any consumer's possession.* Here is a stream of outputs such as some machines, roads, office buildings, bridges, airports, not to mention smaller objects such as office furniture and office typewriters. These goods are obviously also part of our gross domestic product, but they are not consumers' goods. We give them a special name—*investment goods* or *capital goods*—and we will soon see that they play a vital role in determining our economic well-being. To physical investment goods also should be added outputs of educational skills in schools and the knowledge produced by research and development, together often called *human capital.*

The macro view also enables us to see a rather surprising thing about the two branches of output. It is that each stream supports a different part of the economy. The flow of consumers' goods obviously goes to restore the working strength and well-being of the nation's households. Without it, we would perish in a few weeks. But the investment flow of output also plays a restorative function. Investment output replenishes and renews the capital wealth of the nation. The flow of investment output terminates in repairs to and extensions of our system of dams and roads, assembly lines and warehouses, lathes and drill presses, farm equipment, apartment houses, skills and knowledge. If that stream of output dried up, we would not perish as quickly as if consumer output disappeared, but our productive strength would soon wither, and by degrees we would be forced back to the level of an underdeveloped, then of a primitive, society.

GDP, then, consists of two main kinds of output—consumption goods and investment goods. The roughly $8 trillion that gross domestic product amounted to in 1997, for instance, is nothing but the total sales value of these two basic kinds of output. It may help to think of the river of production as passing through the checkout counters of an immense supermarket. The sales ticket on each item is rung up on a cash register. After a year of ringing up the checkouts, a total is taken of the tapes. That's GDP for the year.*

---

*We add a footnote you may never use—but that one day you might want badly. Until quite recently, the name we gave our total production was gross *national* product, or GNP, not gross *domestic* product, or GDP. The difference is minor: GDP measures the value of all goods and services produced within the United States, regardless of whether the producer is a U.S. firm or a foreign one located here, or whether it is an American worker or a national residing here. In contrast, gross *national* product—GNP—measures the value of the output of all U.S. citizens, regardless of whether they are working in the United States or abroad. Almost all countries use GDP these days, but we only switched

*   *   *

A few things ought to be noticed about this GDP. One of them is that the flow of output through the checkout counter is comprised of both public and private goods and services. Take the flow of consumption, for example. Consumption goods or services, as the words indicate, are goods that we consume or use up, usually in a fairly short period. Most consumption goods are bought by private households for their personal use—food or clothing, for instance, or services such as movie admissions or legal advice. But some consumption outputs are bought by local or state or federal governments. Firefighters' services, for example, resemble the professional services of lawyers or oil-well firefighters, but they are part of public consumption, not private. This is true even though households in the end get the benefit of the firefighters' performances: The "person" who pays the bill for their services is the state.

The same division into private and public can be observed if we look at investment. Investment goods typically last a long time and are replaced when they wear out, as is the case with a factory. But this is also true of a road or a dam or a city-owned incinerator plant. These are investment goods too, but they are public, not private. Some investment goods, such as skills and knowledge, are bought by both the public and private sectors.

While we are concerning ourselves about public expenditure, one additional thing should be noted. It is that very large and important flow of government spending, mainly federal, called transfer payments. This is the stream of payments mentioned in Chapter Four mainly for "safety net" purposes: Social Security payments, health care, unemployment compensation, help for the disabled or disadvantaged, plus subsidies of various kinds. Government transfers came to more than $1.1 trillion in 1997, equal to about 14 percent of GDP.

Yet when we add up GDP we do not include transfer payments in it! This is because transfers, as the name indicates, are payments made for social purposes, not because the recipients perform a useful service. Here is the difference: when we pay our cleaning bill, we transfer

---

from GNP to GDP a few years ago. Thus, if you are looking up statistics of total output of a few years back, you are likely to find them identified as GNP. Fortunately, for most purposes the difference in dollar sums between GDP and GNP is very small. Anyway, now you know.

money to someone who has done work for us. So too, when we pay taxes to help finance schools or fire departments or even armies, we also pay individuals who perform services on our behalf. But the portion of the taxes we pay that is used to provide income to individuals who cannot find work, or are too infirm to support themselves, or who have reached retirement, is not a reward for effort. It is a form of institutionalized social responsibility that has become part of every advanced nation. It is, in fact, the public equivalent of private charity. *But because no direct production takes place in exchange for a transfer payment, such as a Social Security check, they are simply left out when we calculate GDP.** The same is true for gambling outlays, or the buying of stocks and bonds, or disaster relief. These are all large and important flows of spending, but they do not reflect the activity of production that GDP sets out to measure. Consumption is being transferred from one person to another but additional output is not being produced.

When GDP is actually calculated by Commerce Department statisticians, the river of output is imagined to pass through not one, but four checkout lines. One of them rings up the total of personal consumption expenditures, all of them made by private households. A second register totals up all the private domestic investment output of the country, mainly business plant and equipment and new homes for families. A third checkout line keeps track of all government output—federal, state, and local—whether for consumption or investment purposes. There is really no reason why we do not separate the stream of public output into a consumption and an investment branch, as we do with private output, and it might help us better understand the government's place in the economy if we did. But we don't, so school lunch programs and new subway trackage are put together in one government output figure.

Along the same lines, educational spending is classified as consumption in all official statistics, although it is really a mixture of consumption and investment. In the same way, the hardware part of research and

---

*Another way of looking at it is that a transfer payment takes money from some Americans and transfers it to others—for example, from taxpayers to the unemployed. But government itself does not "spend" the money, unlike the case with government spending that enters GDP, such as road-building or military expenditures.

development spending gets classified as investment, but the people costs of R&D do not. This occurs because when investment was first defined in the GDP statistics it had a bricks-and-mortar connotation that is no longer true but is still embedded in much of our official statistics.*

Finally, there is a fourth counter, where we ring up all the U.S. production that is sold abroad and where we subtract all the foreign production that is bought here. If we sell more than we buy, there is a positive "export balance" as part of GDP. If, as in recent years, we buy more abroad than we sell there, there is a negative export balance—a net stream of purchasing power that wends its way abroad.

Thus the GDP figure we read about is the sum of four separate tallies (involving hundreds and hundreds of detailed reports and estimates) of our national output. In 1996, for example, the four tallies were:

GDP: 1996	$ billion
Personal consumption expenditure	5,151
Private domestic investment outlays	1,117
Government purchases	1,406
Export balance	-99
Total Gross Domestic Product	*7,576*

There is one last matter. In adding up our GDP, government statisticians do not record the value of every good that is produced each time it is sold. If they did, they would have to add up the value of a bushel of wheat to a grain elevator, the grain sold to a miller, the flour sold to a baker, the bread sold to a supermarket, and, finally, the loaf sold to a consumer. This would be a much bigger figure than the value of the final loaf—and yet the value of the loaf clearly contains the payments that have been previously made to the baker, the miller, the grain elevator, and the farmer!

Following along this line, statisticians only keep track of final goods, not of intermediate ones. As we would imagine, each of the checkout

*Recently, a start has been made in separating U.S. statistics into government investment and government consumption, as most European nations do. As we shall see later on, such a separation is essential if we are to formulate an intelligent plan for government spending.

counters tots up one category of these final goods: consumers' goods, investment goods, government output, and net exports.

WHAT DOES GDP TELL US?

It should be pretty clear by now what GDP consists of. What is not yet so clear is how important it is. Does the size of GDP tell us accurately how well off we are? Is it good if GDP goes up, and bad if it goes down?

The answer is yes and no. The yes part is easy to understand. When the value of production rises, more people are likely to be employed. When the value of total output increases, more incomes are sure to be received. So there is an evident connection between the size of GDP and the level of employment and of national incomes. The size of GDP also serves as a general measure of the amount of goods and services that we can buy, individually and collectively. That is why, all things considered, a rising GDP is always welcome, and a falling one unwelcome.

Yet GDP is also a flawed and deceiving measure of our well-being, and we should understand the weaknesses as well as the strengths of this most important single economic indicator.

To begin with, GDP deals in dollar values, not in physical units. Therefore, we have to correct it for inflation. As we know from the last chapter, trouble arises when we compare the GDP of one year with that of another to determine whether or not the nation is better off. If prices in the second year are higher, GDP will appear larger even though the actual volume of output is unchanged or even lower. Thus, GDP is an accurate indicator of well-being only if we can accurately take out the inflation factor in comparing one year with another. Can we? Well, partly, but not perfectly. There is always a margin of uncertainty in comparing the "real" GDP of today with that of yesterday.

A second weakness of GDP also involves its inaccuracy as an indicator of "real" trends over time. The difficulty revolves around changes in the quality of goods and services. In a technologically advanced society, goods usually are improved over time, and new goods are being introduced constantly. At the same time, in an increasingly high-density society, the quality of other services may be lessened: an airplane trip today is certainly preferable to one of thirty years ago, but a subway ride is not.

Historically, government statisticians have tried to adjust GDP statistics for quality improvement in the manufacturing sector, but have completely ignored quality improvements in the service sector. That practice did not generate significant measurement errors when goods dominated the GDP and were the driver of economic growth. But it has become a greater and greater source of error now that services are 70 percent of the GDP and increasingly the generator of economic growth.

Consider the ability to withdraw money from your bank account in the middle of the night from an ATM machine. That ability is an improvement in the quality of banking services; but it has never been recorded as such in our GDP statistics. By not measuring improvements in the quality of services we underestimate the real growth of the economy and overestimate the rate of inflation. What we measure as price increases in the service sector are often the costs of providing higher quality services.

Traditionally the GDP is divided into agricultural, mining, construction, manufacturing, and service sectors. It is important to understand that the service sector is not a homogeneous sector in the way that these other sectors are. Historically the service sector was simply what was left over after these other sectors had been defined. It includes high-tech, capital-intensive activities that make products such as nuclear power along with low-tech, labor-intensive activities such as dog walkers. Airlines and the local barber are lumped together. The service sector pays some of the highest wages in the nation to medical doctors and investment bankers, yet on average is a low-wage sector. Statistically it is just too heterogeneous to be interesting. In the not too distant future our GDP accounts undoubtedly will undergo a major revision as services are brought into our statistics of output in a more sophisticated way.

A third difficulty with GDP lies in its blindness to the ultimate use of production. If in one year GDP rises by a billion dollars, owing to an increase in expenditure on education, and in another year it rises by the same amount because of a rise in cigarette production, the figures in each case show the same amount of growth. Even output that turns out to be wide of the mark or totally wasteful—such as the famous Edsel car that no one wanted, or military weapons that are obsolete from the moment they appear—all count as GDP.

The problems of environmental or social deterioration add still another difficulty. Some types of GDP growth directly contribute to pollution—cars, paper, or steel production, for example. Other types of GDP growth are necessary to stop pollution—sewage disposal plants or the production of clean internal-combustion engines. Locks and burglar alarms are measured as positive additions to output when in fact the need for them points to a reduction in the quality of life. In the GDP, prisons and hotels are equivalent.

Thus our conventional measure of GDP makes no distinction among such outputs. For instance, the cleaning bills we pay to undo damage caused by smoke from the neighborhood factory become part of GDP, although cleaning our clothes does not increase our well-being but only brings it back to what it was in the first place. In the same way, our GDP also does not count unpaid work effort within the family. As a result when a mother enters the paid labor force, the measured increase in GDP is bigger than the real increase in output since no subtraction has been made for the output that is no longer produced at home!

Finally, GDP does not indicate anything about the distribution of goods and services among the population. Societies differ widely in how they allocate goods and services among their populations: compare highly egalitarian Sweden and highly inegalitarian Mexico, whose total GDPs are roughly the same. Thus, to know the size of GDP or the level of GDP per capita is to know nothing about the social consequences of that GDP. A rich country may have lots of poverty that it is indifferent to, or perhaps impotent to correct. A poor country can produce a few millionaire families: some Indian princes used to receive their weight in gold from their peoples each year.

All these doubts and reservations (and some others we've left unmentioned) should instill in us a caution against using GDP as if it were a clear-cut measure of social contentment or happiness. Economist Edward Denison once remarked that perhaps nothing affects national economic welfare so much as the weather, which certainly does not get into the GDP accounts! Hence, although one country may have a GDP per capita higher than another, it does not mean that life is better there. It may be worse.

Yet, with all its shortcomings, GDP is still the simplest way we possess of summarizing the overall level of activity of the economy. If we want to examine a country's welfare, we had better turn to specific social indicators of how long its people live, how healthy they are, how cheaply they can obtain good medical care, how varied and abundant is their diet, and so forth—none of which we can tell from GDP figures alone. But we are not always interested in welfare, partly because it is too complex to be summed up in a single measure. For instance, the indices of health care or crime are better in Japan than in the United States, but not the index of living space per person. There are lots of other data that could be consulted.

Yet when we reach that famous bottom line that economists like to talk about, the changes in GDP are still the best measure we have of what is happening to the level of economic activity, and the GDP has the great value of being at everyone's fingertips. Thus it has become, for better or worse, the world's economic yardstick. Fortunately, GDP is also not a static concept. The precise measurement techniques used to construct it have evolved slowly over time, and it will remain a central theme in the economic lexicon for a long time to come.

SIX

Saving and Investing

Why does GDP fluctuate? Accidents of weather or natural disasters aside, why does the river of production run fast one year and slow the next? The question begins to take us into the real purpose of macroeconomic inquiry. Now that we know what GDP is, we want to know why it behaves the way it does, cycling up and down.

A good way to begin is to look once again at the flow of output, this time paying heed not to the actual production of goods and services that get tallied by the Commerce Department statisticians, but at the buyers standing at those checkout counters ready to take delivery of the nation's production. As we would expect, the nation's households are gathered at the consumption counter, its business firms cluster around the investment counter, government agencies make up the buyers at the government counter, and foreign firms and individuals and governments wait at the last counter.

Looking at GDP from this perspective, we see it not so much as a stream of goods, but as a flow of buying power, of expenditure, of demand. Each and every good that moves along the river of output is drawn by someone's willingness to spend money for it. Money makes goods move. As Adam Smith said, "Money is the great wheel of circulation."

Switching our attention from production to buying brings us much closer to an answer as to why the level of GDP fluctuates. Output fluctuates because the demand for it rises and falls. This is not the *only* reason why production varies—droughts and earthquakes, strikes and technical hang-ups, government regulations may also alter the level of production, as well as the adverse effects of taxation on the incentive to produce. But even the most probusiness economist will agree that demand—the willingness and ability to buy goods—is essential for the river of production to flow. Thus, the way to begin our investigation is by examining where demand comes from and what makes it rise or fall.

HOUSEHOLD SAVING, BUSINESS SPENDING

We turn to the first checkout counter, where the nation's households are queuing up to buy the national output of consumers' goods and services. Where does the flow of household spending come from?

The answer is that it comes in the main from household earnings—the wages, salaries, rents, dividends, profits, or whatever other payments householders have received from the work they have performed. It also comes from transfer payments, such as Social Security checks. The flow of spending can be augmented, at least for a while, if households actually draw down their savings accounts or sell assets such as stocks or bonds, but people rarely do that to buy ordinary consumers' goods. Finally, the flow can be also augmented by borrowing, so that in any one year some households will spend more than their current incomes—often the case when there is an expensive purchase such as a car.*

Just the same, when we look at the sum total of all household incomes and compare it with the total of all household expenditures for consumers' goods, we discover that households as a whole—a "sector," economists say—regularly save (don't spend) some portion of their incomes. Over time American savings has fallen from about 9 percent in the early 1970s to about 5 percent in 1996. That is, even *after* households have borrowed, used their credit cards and charge accounts and all the rest, they still take in more money than they lay out.

Savings rates vary greatly among countries. Until the recent Asian crisis, Singapore households had to put almost half their incomes into a government savings plan. Japanese families saved well over 10 percent, Italian households twice that. To a small extent, these differences flow from what economists call differences in *time preference.* Rates of

---

*Household spending includes autos but not houses. The latter are counted as *investment* goods, not as consumer goods.

time preference refer to the willingness of individuals to postpone their consumption today in order to consume more tomorrow.

While rates of time preference undoubtedly vary from group to group, the huge differences that we see among countries don't so much reflect these differences as they do differences in the ease with which individuals can borrow to finance consumption purposes. If borrowing is discouraged, as in societies where home mortgages and credit cards are not easily available, or where government rules require large down payments and quick repayment, saving rates will be much higher, even though the citizens of the countries may have very similar rates of time preference. This probably explains why the Japanese saved so much and Americans save so little out of their respective incomes.

There is no difficulty in understanding where the demand comes for the part of GDP that is made up of consumers' goods. All of it comes directly out of the earnings and transfer incomes of households, supplemented by their borrowings. In fact, looking at GDP from the macro viewpoint, the question that occurs to us is not where consumer demand comes from, but what happens to the 5 percent of household earnings that do *not* get returned to the economy but are instead saved.

That question turns our attention to the next checkout counter, where investment goods are bought by private business. Just as the household sector buys its everyday consumption goods mainly out of its earnings, so the business sector buys its ordinary day-to-day requirements from the money it regularly takes in from its sales. We can picture the nation's business as a gigantic household, buying its needed services of labor and its inputs of raw materials or semifinished goods from the receipts it takes in by selling its finished output.

There is, however, a critical difference between the household sector and the business sector. It is that the business sector does not normally save some portion of its receipts. *On the contrary, it spends more than it takes in through its sales.* That idea is so important that it warrants saying a second time. The normal, regular, healthy, and even necessary behavior of the business community as a whole is to lay out more money for wages, salaries, raw materials, semifinished goods, land, and capital than the total amount it takes in by selling its own output.

When we put it this way, business behavior sounds very unsafe. How can even the largest corporation afford to lay out more, year after year, than it takes in from its sales? The answer is that over and above its normal revenues, business takes in additional financial revenues by borrowing from banks or by selling its stocks and bonds. These additional resources—the new capital funds it raises—are also spent, not to pay the regular running expenses of firms, but to pay for capital improvements. AT&T does not use the proceeds of its bond issues to pay the wages of its phone operators, but to pay for the additions to its phone lines, its new buildings, its satellites.

Thus the process of saving and investing goes directly to the central issue of macroeconomics. Household and other savings are "acquired" by the business sector to finance the building of new capital goods. In turn, spending on investment goods becomes a primary means by which we increase our productivity (output per hour of work) and thereby cause GDP to increase. Here is the first explanation of how GDP grows and why it fluctuates. The explanation is important enough to set apart:

1. Gross domestic product grows because savings that originate in the household sector are converted into capital equipment.
2. GDP fluctuates because the process of transforming savings into investment is not always smooth or steady.

HOW THE SECTORS INTERLOCK

These critical relationships may come as something of an anticlimax, because everyone knows that savings and investing lie at the heart of economic growth, even if the process is not often described so precisely. But there are aspects of the saving and investing process that everyone does not know, and it is these to which we now turn. Let's begin with saving. We think of saving as putting money in a bank or in a financial institution of some other kind. What we do not often realize is that saving has two quite distinct meanings. The first of these is indeed putting money aside and not spending it. The second is letting go of or investing those resources.

Putting money in a bank or in a pension plan or a new issue of stock has the *immediate* effect of creating a gap or a shortfall in demand. The gap arises because some of the earnings that householders have received from firms or government will not be returned to circulation as part of the consumption flow. In a word, saving means not consuming. As we have just seen, this doesn't mean that those savings remain permanently removed from circulation. We can picture householders on the consumption queue, lending or otherwise transferring their savings to the businessmen standing at the investment queue. But until the transfer is actually made, through the banking system or the stock market, saving means only that householders have taken some of their earnings and decided not to use it for buying consumption goods.

We'll return in a moment to the question of getting the money into the hands of the business queue. Meanwhile, however, we must also understand that saving is more than just a financial matter. It is also an action that frees labor and resources from the production of consumer goods and thereby makes them available for producing other goods.

An illustration may help us see this. Suppose, for example, that businessmen decided to double their investment spending in anticipation of a boom. Or suppose that the government wanted to double its military spending in anticipation of a war. It is obvious that such an increase in the spending of the business or government sectors would send the price of labor and of other materials shooting upward, as business and government struggled to get their hands on the labor force and the materials they needed. That would result in higher costs, and could start an inflationary scramble.

In fact, there is only one way in which a large increase in investment or government spending can possibly be undertaken without such a scramble: the resources and labor they need must be made available to them. One way in which this can be done is by taxing—simply taking away spending power from households and giving it to government. But industry has no taxing power. For business, the only way that resources can be made available on a large scale is for them to be voluntarily relinquished by the household sector. We call that process of voluntary relinquishment *saving*. Of course, householders may be tempted to give up their spending by all sorts of financial inducements from banks or other institutions, but it is a voluntary, not a forced act nonetheless.

Thus, the really constructive aspect of saving is not so much its financial side, which merely creates a gap in spending, but its "real" side—giving up a claim on land and labor and capital for the immediate enjoyments they could produce.

This leads to the last vital link in the chain. The released resources must now be taken up and put to use by the business sector. If they are not put to use, the shortfall in demand created by the financial act of saving will simply hurt consumer sales, without any compensation in the sales of other goods, and the labor and other resources released by households will stand idle. Thus the last, most active and creative part of the whole process lies in the decisions of the business sector to undertake the act of capital formation. As we will see in our next chapter, this is inherently a risky and uncertain process.

So saving and investment have implications and meanings less familiar to us than the general recognition that there is a saving-and-investing process at work. Indeed, there is one unfamiliar aspect that we can now see is the key to how the macro system works. It is that *economic growth takes place through the coordination and cooperation of the sectors.*

As ordinary participants in the economy, we never think of coordinating our activity with that of anyone else, much less that of a sector. Nor does any businessman think of cooperating with the household or any other sector when he undertakes plans for an addition to his establishment. Both simply look at market prices when they decide to consume or invest. Prices tell the economic actors what to do—it's time to make a good purchase or it's time to make a good investment. Such indirect coordination through market prices is what Adam Smith called the Invisible Hand. It is by such a continuous coordination and cooperation that the system grows—and it is by imperfections in the interplay of the sectors that it falters.

The interplay can be stated very simply:

1. A gap in demand—in any sector—must be offset by additional demand in another sector. If this act of coordination does not take place, there will be a fall in demand, a decline in GDP, unemployment, and trouble.
2. An increase in investment or in government spending, assuming there is reasonably full employment, requires that resources be made available to the expanding sector. This can only be accomplished by taxing or by voluntary saving.
3. If expanding sectors spend more than the savings made available to them, there will be an upward pressure on the system, and the possibility of inflation. If the active sectors spend less than the flow of savings, there will be a downward pressure on the system, and the possibility of a recession.

Of course, this is not the whole story of boom and bust, inflation and recession. We have not touched on such critical matters as money, productivity, or the role of government. But a first *structural* understanding of the economy has begun to emerge. We can see that growth does not just happen but comes about from a mutually supportive interaction of the sectors of the system. How that interaction is brought about and how it can be corrected when it fails to achieve the right result are the problems that will occupy us over many pages to come.

THE GOVERNMENT ENTERS

But we are not yet done with the checkout counter. We have seen how demand for GDP arises because households spend most of their earnings and businesses spend most of their own revenues plus the savings they have acquired from the household sector. But we have not yet observed what happens at the government checkout station or at the counter where foreigners line up.

Government first. At first glimpse there is an immediate resemblance between the government sector and the sectors of business or of private households. Considering government as a collection of local, state, and federal purchasing agencies, we can see that the sector buys its goods and services with its everyday receipts—its tax revenues—just as businesses and families spend their normal receipts. In an important way, however, the receipts of government are different from those of households and businesses. With rare exceptions, government does not sell its outputs, however useful they may be. Toll roads or the fees for landing at an airport are exceptions to the general rule that government distributes its services without charge. Therefore it has to assure its income by some other means, and so the government simply commandeers a portion of household or business income. The word *commandeer* may seem extreme, but we must recognize that taxes are not like ordinary charges. A household or a business may refuse to purchase the output of another household or business, but they cannot refuse to purchase the output of government. Taxes are a compulsory payment.

On the other hand, it is well to bear in mind that taxes are also the expression of the will of the electorate, however clumsily that will may be expressed. Moreover, we should bear in mind that government provides one absolutely essential service in exchange for its taxes—a service without which no household or business could earn a cent. That is the service of providing law and order and protecting property rights. "It is only under the shelter of the civil magistrate," wrote Adam Smith, "that the owner of . . . valuable property . . . can sleep a single night in security."*

Thus there is a profound difference between the political roles of the public and private sectors. But we must also recognize that there is a striking resemblance between the sectors with regard to their economic cooperation and coordination. Suppose, for example, that the household sector creates a demand gap by making its normal savings, and that the business sector, for whatever reason, fails to offset that gap by borrowing or gathering the savings through new stock issues and the like. *Could not the government borrow these unused savings and close the demand gap by spending them for public purposes, such as public investment?*

The answer, of course, is that it can. If there is a demand gap that must be "closed" by investment spending, what difference does it make if the investment is for a communications satellite owned by AT&T or one owned by the government, or a rail line owned by Santa Fe or owned by Amtrak, or a private utility plant or a public one, a private factory or a public dam? There is no difference. What is essential is that the savings of one sector be spent by another, or that the investment spending of one sector be saved by another.

Of course this is not the end to the matter. There is room for a great deal of controversy as to which investment or consumption activities the government should pursue and which it should not. There is room for debate as to whether the government can safely spend its borrowings for consumption purposes—Social Security, for instance—that do not generate future returns. There is a great deal of controversy as to whether the government may inadvertently "crowd out" private enterprise when it expands its activities, a matter we will look into later.

So the question of the role of government is not easily settled. What *is* easily settled, however, is that the government sector can play exactly the same investing role as the business sector. Government can use its borrowing powers just like business to offset a shortfall in spending elsewhere. Whether it *should* do these things is a question we will have to consider further. But it is important to see that the govern-

*Wealth of Nations, p. 670.

ment, as a sector, can—indeed, must—coordinate its activities with other sectors. No economist, conservative or radical, would deny that.

One last source of demand should be looked at quickly. This is the foreign checkout counter, where overseas buyers provide demand for U.S. output by taking delivery of grain and computers and jet planes and machinery, and where foreign sellers deliver coffee and ores and oil and Toyotas to waiting American buyers. The workings of the foreign-demand part of GDP are more complicated than those of the other sectors, since they depend upon income in other countries and exchange rates between different currencies. We will come back to this aspect later, in Chapter Eighteen. For the time being, however, we can simply note its presence, while we concentrate our attention on the three domestic counters—households, business, and government.

We have come to see that saving-and-investing—we hyphenate the process to emphasize its essential linkage—is the key to economic growth and economic fluctuation. It is the key to growth because investment is the activity by which we lay down the equipment, skills, and knowledge that makes us more productive. In two centuries we have moved from Adam Smith's simple pin factories to multibillion semiconductor manufacturing plants, in the process mutliplying by factors of ten and a hundred and a thousand the material goods that can be fashioned in an hour of work.

Saving-and-investing is also the key to fluctuations in GDP, because the process does not go on at a steady rate, but faster or slower as various factors alter the flow of saving—or more usually, as they alter the prospects for investment. That is a matter we will examine in our next chapter.

But first, there remains one vitally important point to remember. *Demand is the driving force of the economy.* It is the volume of total spending—the spending of households on consumption goods, of business firms on capital goods, of government on its consumption and investment purchases, and of foreigners on net exports—that supplies the day-by-day stimulus for our gross domestic production. When demand falters for any reason, GDP falters, and with it employment and incomes. But why should it falter? That's the question to which we now turn.

SEVEN

Passive Consumption, Active Investment

Of all the forms of economic behavior, household spending and saving are the most familiar. Who has not fretted about adding to a savings account or life insurance or investments? Who has not experienced the tug-of-war between the desire to live it up—"buy now, pay later"—and the desire to provide for the proverbial rainy day or college education or retirement or whatever?

These small dramas of deciding between spending and saving are played out each year in millions of households, each of which is convinced that its circumstances are unique. In fact, when we take the household sector as an entirety, the dramas come to an astonishingly predictable collective conclusion. As we have already noted in our last chapter, households altogether regularly spend about ninety-five cents of every dollar they receive and save about five cents. As we have seen, this makes American families spendthrifts compared with many other countries. Later on, when we investigate the question of productivity, we will come back to these differences in national savings rates.

THE PROPENSITY TO CONSUME

Right now, while we are still concentrating on the dynamics of GDP, the thing to bear in mind is that national savings rates—*propensities* to save, economists call them—change only slowly. Their short-run constancy allows economists to predict with a high degree of certainty the amount of consumption (or its counterpart, saving) that will be associated with any given level of household income.

Taken all together, this flow of consumption spending is about two thirds as large as GDP. That is, household buying provides the demand that brings forth two thirds of our national production. About 30 percent of this household buying is for "nondurables"—perishable items such as food and clothing and the like. A slightly larger stream of buying is for a variety of consumer services, ranging from air travel to restaurants. The remainder is for long-lasting items, such as automobiles or household appliances, called consumer durables. As we would imagine, the demand for durables is much more volatile than that for nondurables: people must eat, but they can postpone buying a TV set. Hence, even within the broad flow of household buying there are sub-flows that are extremely steady and others that are highly dynamic.

Just the same, *the essential characteristic of consumer spending as a whole is its dependable, predictable nature.* Give an economist reason to believe that next year's GDP will be so-and-so many billions, and he or she will be able to tell you within a percentage point or two how large consumer buying will be. It's on this basis that various economic models permit businesses to make forecasts with regard to general market prospects.*

There are, in fact, only three circumstances in which consumer spending does not behave in this passive fashion. One of these is wartime. As we would expect, during most wars consumer spending is deliberately held back by heavy taxes to make room for swelling military expenditure. During World War II, for example, consumption was squeezed back by heavy taxes to barely more than half of GDP. Coming out of the Great Depression consumption spending was very low, and as a result dollar expenditures for consumption rose all during the war, but GDP itself rose so much faster that the share of consumption fell markedly: Consumers took a smaller share of a much bigger pie. During the Vietnam War military expenses for that conflict were not compensated by taxes to roll back consumption and the excess demand for goods and services ignited a subsequent inflation.

A second circumstance in which consumption departs from its nor-

---

*Of course, it is one thing to forecast that total consumer spending will be so-and-so many hundred billion dollars, and another thing to predict the particular tiny eddy in which your specific product will be carried along.

mal propensity is during extreme depressions. There are needs that must be filled to keep going; and when incomes fall because of unemployment, afflicted families may beg, borrow, and if necessary steal to keep body and soul together. Certainly, during bad times household savings are eaten up rapidly. Hence consumption tends to be a larger *proportion* of GDP, even though the actual amount of consumer spending is down: the GDP pie is smaller, but the consumption portion takes a larger share of the diminished pie.

Finally, the propensity-to-consume relationship—to give it its proper economic name—may depart from the norm during inflationary periods. The reason is that families begin to feel the inflationary itch—the decision to buy ahead of their normal requirements in order to get things before they become more expensive. Thus inflation can give rise to a surge of buying at the expense of normal savings.

Economists have spent a great deal of time investigating the propensity to consume. For our purposes, however, the dependable and predictable behavior of normal consumption has one simple but central implication. It is that consumption spending—the broad flow of household expenditure that buys up two thirds of GDP—is *not a driving force in our economy, but a driven one.* For all its size, it is not the engine of GDP. It is the caboose.

To be sure, we have to be a little careful about this assertion. We have noted already that consumer spending on durable items such as cars is much more volatile than spending for nondurables or services, and swings in durable spending can pack a substantial economic wallop. In 1974 and again in 1979, for example, consumers held back on auto purchases for fear of gasoline shortages, and each time the effect on auto sales alone had an impact on GDP.

Just the same, these are exceptions to the rule. During the normal course of things, no matter how intense their wants may be, consumers lack the spendable income to translate their wants into actions. They have desires, but demand requires more than desire: it must be backed up by available cash.

This highlights an extremely important point. Wants and appetites alone do not drive the economy upward; if they did, we should experience a more impelling demand in depressions, when people are hungry, than in booms, when they are well off. Hence the futility of those who urge the cure of depressions by suggesting that consumers should buy more! There is nothing consumers would rather do than buy more, if only they could. Let us not forget, furthermore, that consumers are at all times being cajoled and exhorted to increase their expenditures by the multibillion-dollar pressures exerted through the advertising industry.

The trouble is, however, that consumers cannot buy more unless they have more income to buy with. Of course, for short periods they can borrow or they may sharply reduce their rate of savings temporarily, but each household's borrowing capacity or accumulated savings is limited, so that once these bursts are over, the steady habitual ways of saving and spending are apt to reassert themselves.

Thus it is clear that in considering the consumer sector we study a part of the economy that, however ultimately important, is not in itself the source of major changes in activity. Consumption mirrors changes elsewhere in the economy, but it does not initiate the greater part of our long-run economic fortunes or misfortunes. This is a bit of economic insight worth remembering.

INVESTMENT DEMAND

Consumer buying, we have seen, gives the impetus to about two thirds of GMP. Where does the rest come from? We already know that it originates in the other buying queues: businesses seeking to build more capital or to spend more on R&D; government buying various public outputs; foreigners taking American goods and services.

Investment is the queue that we need to examine next. But investment is not as familiar an activity as consumption, so we must take a moment to clarify our economic vocabulary.

What most people mean by investing is buying stocks or bonds. But that is not exactly what economists mean by the term. They mean the counterpart to the "real" act of saving. The real act of saving, we remember, was to release resources that could have been consumed to allow them to be redirected to investment. The real act of investment is to put these resources to work creating capital goods.

This real act of investing may or may not require the purchase of stocks or bonds. When we buy an ordinary stock or bond on the stock exchange, we usually buy it from someone who has owned it previously. Therefore, our personal act of investment becomes, in the economic view of things, merely a transfer of claims without any direct bearing on the creation of new wealth. **A** pays **B** cash and takes his General Motors stock; **B** takes **A**'s cash and doubtless uses it to buy stock from **C**. But the transactions among **A** and **B** and **C** in no way alter the actual amount of real capital in the economy.

Only when we buy newly issued shares or bonds, and then only when their proceeds are directly allocated to new equipment or plant, does our act of personal financial investment result in the addition of wealth to the community. In that case, **A** buys his stock directly (or through a broker) from General Motors itself. **A**'s cash can now be spent by General Motors for new capital goods, as presumably it will be.

More frequently the individual puts his or her money in the bank and the bank lends businesses funds that they can use for investment. Or wealthy individuals may give their savings to venture capitalists who make direct investments in new start-up businesses.

Thus, much of investment, as economists see it, is a little-known form of activity for the majority of us. This is true not only because real investment is not the same as personal financial investment, but because the real investors of the nation usually act on behalf of an institution other than the familiar one of the household. Boards of directors, chief executives, or small-business proprietors are the persons who decide whether or not to devote business cash to the construction of new facilities or to the addition of inventory, and this decision is very different in character and motivation from the decisions familiar to us as members of the household sector.*

Households buy goods to satisfy their needs and wants, and we have seen how stable is their propensity to consume. But investment is not decided by personal considerations. The only relevant determination that must be made is whether adding to capital goods is expected to yield a good return. Unlike the household sector, the business sector is motivated by profit; "I'm not in business for my health" is the well-known quip. Investment activities are expected to return more funds than were initially used.

The imperative of profits is, of course, central to capitalism—both the source of its dynamic drive and the root of many of its endemic ills. But from the viewpoint of GDP, what is important about profit is that it is always oriented to the future. A firm may be enjoying large profits on

---

*As we noted earlier, the GDP accounts treat the buying of a home as an investment activity, as if the family sets up a "business" of buying a home and then renting it to themselves—but most of us don't think of it that way.

its existing plant and equipment, but if it anticipates no profits from an additional investment, the firm will make no additions to capital. Another firm may be suffering current losses, but if it anticipates a large profit from the production of a new good, it may be able to launch a considerable capital expenditure. The view is always forward, never backward.

There is a sound reason for this anticipatory quality of investment decisions. Typically, the capital goods bought by investment expenditures are expected to last for years and to pay for themselves only slowly. In addition, they are often highly specialized. If capital expenditures could be recouped in a few weeks or months, or even in a matter of a year or two, or if capital goods were transferred from one use to another easily, they would not be so risky. But usually it takes two to four years to go from the drawing board to full-steam production. That means making predictions about the nature of demand well into the future. In addition, it is characteristic of many capital goods that they are durable, with life expectancies of ten or more years, and that they tend to be limited in their alternative uses, or to have no alternative uses at all. You cannot spin cloth in a steel mill or make steel in a cotton mill.

The decision to invest is thus always forward-looking. Even when the stimulus to build is felt in the present, the calculations that determine whether or not an investment will be made necessarily concern the flow of income to the firm in the future. These expectations are inherently much more unstable than the current drives and desires that guide the consumer. Expectations, whether based on guesses or forecasts, are capable of sudden and sharp reversals of a sort rare in consumption spending.

There is a very important consequence of all this for our understanding of GDP. It is that investment is inherently volatile in a way that consumption is not. In the short run, this volatility often expresses itself in sharp swings in inventory buying. We do not ordinarily think of inventories as constituting part of our capital wealth, but they are. A business firm that feels sales are about to rise invests in more finished goods, products ready to sell, or it buys more raw materials and components so that it can increase production levels. The volatility of inventory buying comes about because businesses may increase or decrease inventory purchases rapidly, based on sales expectations. When they increase them, of course they give rise to a quick upswing in the demand for investment goods. When they cut back on inventory purchases, there is an equally sharp letdown in investment demand. Just as an illustration, businesses were working off inventories at the rate of $24 billion a year during the last quarter of 1990. Four quarters later they were accumulating inventories at a rate of $14 billion per year. That was an upward swing of $38 billion in demand for GDP.

The second form of investment instability is related to the longer business cycle, with its irregular sequence of ups and downs. When the outlook for several years ahead is gloomy, investment spending can fall precipitously. During the Great Depression of the thirties, business virtually ceased all expansion and barely replaced its machinery and equipment when it wore out: from 1929 to 1933, when household consumption fell by 41 percent, investment fell by 91 percent. In fact, at the bottom of the Depression it was estimated that one third of all unemployment in the nation was directly attributable to the catastrophic shrinkage in the demand for capital goods. Conversely, when the Depression finally turned around in 1933, consumption rose by somewhat more than half over the next seven years, but investment expanded nine times.

Last, but certainly not least, as a driver of investment is technology. Later in this chapter we will look more carefully into the transformative effects of some—not all—inventions. Here it is enough merely to add technology to the list of elements that give not only vitality but irregularity to investment. Powerful inventions do not come on regular schedules, and when they are slow in arriving, or simply absent, we can only wait until research or ingenuity or sheer luck opens a new field for capital spending.

One further aspect of the investment problem is worth our notice. Investment is not only a driving and potentially destabilizing force in the economy, but its impact is magnified because of what economists call the "multiplier." The idea of the multiplier is simplicity itself. When a change in spending occurs, such as a new investment project, the money laid out for construction workers' wages, materials, and the like does not stop there. The recipients of the first round of investment spending will engage in additional spending of their own. What they buy provides new sales and hence jobs for others. And so initial bursts of spending create secondary and tertiary bursts until the effect is finally dissipated.

By and large economists estimate that the impact of the multiplier over the course of a year is about two. This works downward as well as upward. Thus the contraction in investment spending of $28 billion during 1990 would have given rise to a twofold contraction in incomes throughout the nation, pulling the demand for GDP down by $56 billion, if net exports had not risen by a like amount. And of course when investment rises by, say $10 billion, the country will enjoy an increase of incomes of that original $10 billion plus an additional $10 billion from the multiplier.

Two final and very important conclusions follow from this. First, we have seen that investment is a driving, not a driven, part of the economy. To be sure, as with consumption, investment spending is also influenced by the incomes that businesses receive. Some investment follows the direction of consumer buying, especially accelerations and decelerations in consumption spending. When consumption spending rises, new factories have to be built to service it. But the distinguishing feature of investment, taken as the critical activity of the business sector, is that it is not a caboose, but an engine. It leads the economy.

Second, there is the question of how we explain why investment spending seems to follow some sort of roughly cyclical pattern of years of boom followed by years of bust. William Stanley Jevons suggested in the 1870s that the reason was sunspots. His answer was not as foolish as it may appear. Jevons, an astronomer by training, believed that the well-known ten-year cycle of sunspot activity gave rise to changes in weather, which gave rise to changes in rainfall, which gave rise to changes in crop yields, which gave rise to variations in output. Later research killed the theory by showing that the sunspot cycle did not correspond closely enough to the weather cycle.

Many candidates have been suggested to replace sunspots—bouts of inventory accumulation led by over optimism and followed by the inevitable periods of inventory sell off; overexpansion of bank credit followed by credit squeezes—we'll be looking into how credit is created in Chapters Ten and Eleven ahead. Some cycles have clearly been caused by ups and downs in military spending. But more recently, attention has been less focused on the pendulumlike aspect of cycles and more generally directed to the fundamental forces that make the rate of investment spending—the motor of growth—run now fast, now slow.

THE STOCK MARKET AND INVESTMENT

How does the stock market affect business investment? There are three direct effects. One is that the market traditionally has served as a general barometer of the expectations of the business-minded community as a whole. We say "business-minded" rather than "business" because the demand for, and supply of, securities mainly comes from securities dealers, stockbrokers, and the investing public, rather than from nonfinancial business enterprises themselves. When the market is buoyant, it has been a signal to business that the "business climate" is favorable, and the effect on what Keynes called the "animal spirits" of executives has been to encourage them to go ahead with expansion plans. When the market is failing, on the other hand, spirits tend to be dampened and executives may think twice before embarking on an expansion program in the face of general pessimism.

This traditional relationship is, however, greatly lessened by the growing power of government to influence the trend of economic events. Business once looked to the market as the key signal for the future. Today it looks to Washington. Hence, during the past decade when the stock market has shown wide swings, business investment in plant and equipment has remained basically steady. This reflects the feelings of corporate managers that government policy will keep the economy growing, whatever "the market" may think of events. In 1994 and 1995 the economy grew only slowly, but the stock market boomed nonetheless.

A second direct effect of the stock market on investment has to do with the ease of issuing new securities. One of the ways in which investment is financed is through the issuance of new stocks or bonds whose proceeds will purchase plant and equipment. When the market is rising, it is much easier to float a new issue than when prices are falling. This is particularly true for certain businesses—public utilities, for example—that depend heavily on stock issues rather than retained earnings for new capital. A rising market also makes it easier for venture capitalists to raise funds to lend to new businesses, since venture capital investors expect that within a few years they will be able to sell shares in those new companies at a handsome profit.

Finally, when the market is very low, companies with large retained earnings may be tempted to buy up other companies or buy back their own shares, rather than use their funds for capital expenditure. Financial investment, in other words, may take the place of real investment. This helps successful companies grow but does not directly provide growth for the economy as a whole.

NORMAL AND TRANSFORMATIONAL GROWTH

At the risk of some oversimplification, here is what many economists believe today: Growth is the norm in a capitalist economy. It is the norm because every business, at least every business beyond mom-and-pop size, is constantly trying to make more profits, and to do this they must expand—seek new products, new markets, more efficiency, whatever. Thus, rather as Adam Smith thought, the inner tendency of a free-enterprise economy is toward expansion. Moreover, it tends to extend its growth, not simply to fill up a given need and then quit. What Smith didn't see is that after the market for pins got saturated, someone would get around to inventing safety pins, and then zippers, and then Velcro. As a result of the efforts of capitalists, the opportunity for investment itself grows, at least for a time.

Normal expansion can be helped or hindered by a number of things, some beyond anyone's control, some not. It certainly can be helped by monetary policies that make interest rates low and thereby encourage borrowing for expansion, and it can be slowed down, or brought to a halt, by the opposite—"tight" money. Political developments undoubtedly play their encouraging or discouraging roles. High taxes on profits discourage investment just as low taxes encourage investment. Government expenditures on infrastructure, education, or research and development lower costs and provide the knowledge inputs necessary to generate new products and processes. Government spending—so-called fiscal policy—can help or hinder, as we will see in our next chapter.

But when all is said and done, normal growth, with its ups and downs, is only the background against which the investment drama is played out. As we might anticipate, the most dramatic and important factor seems to be technology—or rather, those particular technological advances that give rise to what economist Edward J. Nell has called "transformational growth." The words refer to remarkable clusters of inventions and innovations that move out what economists call "the production possibility frontier"—that is, the map of feasible and profitable economic activity. In our very first chapter we saw how the steam engine played such a role in the late eighteenth and early nineteenth centuries. A similar impetus was the gift of the railroads that "transformed" the economic map of every nation during the nineteenth century. A third was electrification, bringing power to remote areas, and not less important, into the home. A fourth was the automobile that brought paved highways, gas stations, garages, a whole new tempo to life. In our own time we have seen a fifth in the jet plane and the computer. The computer and the micro-electronics revolution changed the organization of every business, from dry cleaning to multinational corporations; the jet giant brought tourism—by the 1960s the largest single industry in the world—and, even more importantly, the advent of a global economy.

Transformational changes have imparted immense momentum to economic life. But it is the nature of these changes that after a time the new production possibility frontier is occupied and a period of "digestion" follows that of expansion. Then we sit around and wait for a new transformational boom to come.

Will another such boom arrive? Many industries are mentioned as potential sources of another great investment Klondike: biotechnology; new materials such as ceramics; telecommunications; robotics; and (as they say) much, much more. Will these give us transformational growth? That is the question we will look into in our next two chapters.

EIGHT

The Economics of the Public Sector

The economics of households and business presents no special problem. But the economics of the public sector—that's a different matter. Even before they have read about it, many people *know* that they hate the public sector or love it, that government is the cause of our ruination or the source of our salvation.

We will try to cope with that state of mind by taking the problem in two stages. First there are some things to be learned with respect to the economics of the public sector about which virtually all economists, of whatever political stripe, see eye-to-eye. Although these matters are not controversial, they are important and perhaps surprising. They are the aspects of the problem we will attend to in this chapter. Then there are the issues about which liberals and conservatives do not agree. These mainly have to do with government's *effectiveness* in economic affairs. How large are the adverse impacts of taxation on individual economic incentives and what are the merits of government relative to private spending? The debates are not about the manner in which the public sector fits into the GDP. We will present both sides of that debate in chapters to come. But first we must clarify a few basic matters.

WHAT "GOVERNMENT" MEANS

The place to begin is by reminding ourselves of three things we have observed already. The first is that we must distinguish the role of government in the economic process as a buyer of output from its role as a spender of money. The difference, we may remember, lies in those important expenditures called transfer payments, such as Social Security. Many of the disputes about how big government is or how fast it is growing hinge on whether the arguer is talking about government as a buyer or as a spender. In 1996, for example, government (local, state, and federal) bought about 22 percent of GDP. But the amount that government spent was over 40 percent larger, or about 33 percent of GDP, transfers accounting for the difference.

Which measure "counts"? Essentially, the answer depends on what we want to know. Government as a buyer of GDP—a purchaser of defense, education, transportation, and the rest—gives us some idea of the importance of public output as a component of GDP. Transfer payments tell us something quite different. However many billions they may involve, transfer payments do not add a penny to GDP. Transfers are an indication of the extent of the government's role as an agency for the *redistribution* of income, rather than for the production of output. Obviously, it makes sense to keep track of these two forms of government spending separately.

The second distinction is one we have been at pains to emphasize all along—that between federal versus state or local government. *More GDP is bought at the state and local level than at the federal level.* Most of the transfer payments emanate from the federal government, not the states and localities. The box of figures on page 103 shows this clearly. One of the reasons we should bear this division in mind is that the federal government gives a good deal of money to state and local governments. These "grants-in-aid" are, of course, transfer payments. One result is that states and localities can carry out various programs in education, the environment, even in road building they could not otherwise afford. A second result is that the federal government incurs a deficit partly because it supports state and local activity. Erase the transfer from the federal government to cities and states and you will lessen the federal deficit by that amount. Alas, you would simultaneously put the states and localities in a terrific bind. More on that later, too.

Third, we cannot consider government without keeping somewhere in our minds the division between welfare and warfare. Here the purchases-versus-transfers distinction again helps sort out things. Most of federal purchasing of GDP has to do with warfare—in 1996, for example, almost two thirds of the federal contribution to GDP was for military purposes. Despite the cry about an expanding federal government, the federal government buys virtually the same fraction of goods and services from the economy as it did in 1940. It is the states and localities that have vastly enlarged their purchasing, with much larger health and education and transportation programs.

Then why the outcry about the federal government? The reason lies in the tremendous growth in transfer payments. Most of this growth (20 percent since 1960) has gone to finance Social Security, pensions, and health care for the elderly.

Is there a "right" level of government spending? There is no doubt that there exists a very strong antigovernment-spending sentiment in many parts of the nation today. Much of this focuses on the question of waste. Government employees are regularly referred to as "bureau-

HOW BIG IS THE PUBLIC SECTOR?

Here are the numbers that fit into various categories of the public sector.

	(1996) $ Billions
Total Government Spending	2,447
Federal	1,704
State and Local	743
Government Transfers	1,074
Federal	763
State and Local	311
Federal Grants in Aid to State and Local Government	215
Interest Payments, Net Federal	241
Government Purchases	1,181
Federal	462
State and Local	719
Government Consumption	863
Government Investment*	318

*Includes Education and R&D as investment
Source: U.S. Department of Commerce

crats" and government projects as "boondoggles." No doubt both exist, although it might not be too difficult to find their equivalents in the offices of many large companies. And then there is the matter of self-interest. City dwellers do not think that government spends too much on urban problems, but country dwellers do. Country dwellers do not think that government spends too much on agricultural problems, but city dwellers do. The elderly want government spending cut but not their pensions and health care. The young complain about the taxes necessary to pay for the elderly. Couples with children do not want school expenditures cut, but childless couples do.

An economist has no special expertise that enables him or her to resolve these essentially political problems. Economists can speak with some knowledge about the effects of various kinds of spending on transfer payments—for example, the effects of unemployment insurance on making it easier for someone to quit a job—but they cannot really pronounce on whether the effect is good or bad. That is a matter where value judgments come into play.

THE GOVERNMENT AS A SECTOR

However one feels about what government *should* do, it is vital to understand what it *does* do. Economists who disagree sharply about the best government expenditure policies for the country can still agree in their understanding of how the public sector works.

Here the appropriate place to begin is with the difference in motivations that guide public, as contrasted with private, spending. The motivations for the household sector and the business sector are lodged in the free decisions of their respective units. Householders decide to spend or save their incomes as they wish. Similarly, business firms exercise their own judgments on their capital expenditures.

But when we turn to the expenditures of the public sector, we encounter an entirely new motivation. It is no longer fixed habit or profit that determines the rate of spending, but political decisions—that is, the collective will of the people as it is formulated and expressed through their local, state, and federal legislatures and executives.

Thus the presence of an explicit political will gives to the public sector a special significance. This is the only sector whose expenditures and receipts are open to deliberate control. Through public actions such as taxes, expenditures, and regulations, government can exert very important influences on the behavior of households and firms. But we cannot directly alter their economic activity in the manner that is open to us with the public sector.

The basic idea behind modern public-sector macroeconomic policies is simple enough. We have seen that economic recessions have their roots in a failure of the business sector to offset the savings of the economy through sufficient investment. But if a falling GDP is caused by an inadequacy of expenditures in one sector, our analysis suggests an answer. Could not the insufficiency of spending in the business sector be offset by higher spending in another sector, the public sector? Could not the public sector serve as a supplementary avenue for the transfer of savings into expenditure?*

We already know the answer. A demand gap can indeed be closed by transferring savings to the public sector and spending them. We have seen already that so far as the mechanics of the process is concerned, it makes no difference if savings are borrowed by AT&T and spent for a privately owned satellite, or borrowed by the U.S. Treasury and spent for a publicly owned satellite. The politics are different. The effect on business opinion and expectations and confidence may be very different. But speaking strictly in terms of how the sectors operate and cooperate, there is no difference at all. Although economists disagree fiercely about the implications and secondary repercussions of government spending, none would dissent from the proposition that the government's economic activities have to be analyzed as a sector, comparable to the sectors of business or households.

This means that when the government increases its purchases by borrowing and spending, it adds to GDP, just as when households or businesses do the same.†

Conversely, when government decreases its spending, the level of economic activity falls, again just like businesses or households. Finally, if government regularly saves money by taking in more taxes

---

*Of course, another way of stimulating GDP would be to cut taxes in the hope of spurring investment. Here we are not arguing in favor of public spending rather than tax cutting. We are only interested in showing that there is a much closer resemblance between public spending and private investment than is usually recognized.

†When the government spends more money on transfers, it may or may not stimulate GDP, depending upon whether it is giving money to people with a higher propensity to consume than those from whom it is taking money away.

than it spends, thereby running up a budget surplus, it will create a demand gap exactly as when households save their incomes. In that case, business must invest enough to match the savings of both the household and the public sectors, if GDP is not to fall.

DEFICIT SPENDING

So it makes a difference when we see the government's activities as those of a *responsible* sector, not as those of a household or firm making decisions without regard as to their aggregate effects on the level of economic activity. The difference becomes sharpest when we examine that most misunderstood of all the government's activities—deficit spending. Deficit spending means that the government spends more than it takes in through taxes, borrowing the rest. The borrowed sums become part of the government debt, and we frequently hear admonitions about this debt that stem from the tendency to view it as if it were the debt of a single family or enterprise. "The government," we are told, "cannot borrow indefinitely, any more than a family or a firm. A government that incurs a deficit is simply living beyond its means."

Is it true? It *sounds* true. And yet even economists who oppose deficit spending strongly for other reasons would admit that the arguments that equate government with single families or firms are *not* true. Let us take the matter of the deficit. Can the government safely incur a deficit—that is, borrow as well as tax? In Chapter Five, when we first noted how the different queues bought GDP, we saw that the business sector as a whole regularly spent more than its receipts from sales. The difference, we recall, lay in the savings of the household sector that business borrowed to finance its capital outlays.

Now that kind of "excess" spending is certainly not called a deficit by any business firm. When the American Telephone and Telegraph Company or the Exxon Corporation uses the savings of the public to build a new plant and new equipment, it does not show a loss on its annual statement to stockholders, even though its total expenditures on current costs plus those on capital equipment may have been greater than sales. Instead, expenditures are divided into two kinds: one relating current costs to current income, and the other relating expenditures on capital goods to an entirely separate capital account. *Instead of calling the excess of expenditures a deficit, they call it investment.*

Can AT&T or Exxon afford to run "deficits" of the latter kind indefinitely? The answer is yes. The extra earnings from those new investments allow it to pay interest and repay principal on its new bonds. Usually, however, when a bond becomes due, a corporation issues new bonds equal in value to the old ones. It then sells the new bonds and uses the new money it raises to pay off its old bondholders. A successful firm is always seeking to borrow more money to expand its investment base. Between 1929 and today Exxon ran up its long-term debt from $170.1 million in 1929 to over $10 billion. And its credit rating today is as good as, or better than, it was in 1929.

In the aggregate, the business sector is constantly increasing its total indebtedness. In 1975 total corporate long-term debt (debt over one year in maturity) totaled $587 billion. In 1997 it was over $2.6 trillion. Was this safe? The question brings us to a very important point. Borrowing is safe or unsafe, depending to a large degree on what the money is borrowed for. If a company's debt is incurred originally to finance the construction of new plant and equipment, and if the projects are chosen wisely, the rise in debt is likely to be perfectly safe. The growing business debt is then simply the financial face of the company's growing stock of real tangible assets—the machines and equipment that have been purchased with the borrowed funds—and its ability to earn profits. As long as that physical capital is still productive and regularly replaced, why should not the bonds that were sold to pay for it—or new bonds that will replace old ones—still be perfectly sound investments for the individuals or banks or financial companies that wanted a profitable place to invest their savings? That is why most corporate debt has, in fact, generally grown over the years in safety. To be sure, some companies go under, and their bonds lose part—once in a while, all—of their value. But corporate debt as a whole is very safe. If it wasn't, the business system would have collapsed long ago.

But there is also another, different answer. Suppose that corporations borrow funds not to buy capital equipment, but for speculative purposes that turn out badly. Then obviously a growing debt can become a burden on the companies that must pay interest on borrowings that have not produced more income for them—not to speak of a burden on the investors who have invested their savings in nothing.

That is, in fact, what happened during the great merger wave of the 1980s. During those "go-go" years, raiding parties of investors would search out likely targets for a "takeover." The targets were usually big but lackadaisical companies that did not run their operations with an eye on the bottom line. The raiders would then begin to buy stock in the company, usually with the help of a hefty line of credit from a cooperative bank. As soon as a raiding group succeeded in getting enough shares to exercise a controlling voice in the company's affairs, it would install a new management to complete the coup. The new management would thereupon issue very high-interest bonds, using the proceeds to pay back their indebtedness to the bank. It would also strip the company of its best assets, leaving the corporate shell with massive amounts of debt that was not backed by productive assets. These so-called junk bonds then became a burden both on the company and on the incautious investors who had bought them. During these merger mania years, the total volume of corporate debt doubled, and the cost of meeting interest came to absorb 90 percent of all after-tax income of American corporations.

PRIVATE VERSUS PUBLIC DEBTS

Is there a moral in this for the federal deficit? There are two. The first is that the government sector, like the business sector, also can justify its rising debt in terms of an increasing stock of real assets—dams and roads, skills and knowledge, and the like. All through the 1980s, federal investment-type outlays—the analog of private investment—ran at levels roughly equal to the deficit. According to the Office of Management and Budget, such government expenditures amounted to an estimated $581 billion over the fiscal years 1984–1986, close to the total deficit of $624 billion racked up over the same period. If these growth-creating expenditures had not been lumped together with other government spending, we would have had almost no "deficit." Instead, we would have designated these expenditures as public investment, which is indeed what they were, and we would have thought it just as proper to finance them by borrowing as we think it proper to finance private investment by borrowing.

In that case the nation would not have wasted its energies and raised its blood pressure over the misleading question of whether its deficit was too large, but would have argued over the very real and important issue of how much public investment we wanted, and of what kind.

Likewise in the 1990s we should be debating not whether the government may or may not run a deficit, but whether its expenditures in excess of revenue reflect investment or consumption.

The second moral is that we do not run our government affairs in this sensible way because we do not separate government spending into an investment and a consumption category. Instead we lump all government spending into a single flow called "G" (for government), and assume that all of G is used for consumption. If we separated G into expenditures for government investment and government consumption, we would then be able to see exactly how much larger our borrowing was than the amount that could be justified by growth-promoting purposes. If we were running up debt to pay for public consumption, not investment, we could then indeed allow our blood pressure to rise, while we made a real effort to finance our government consumption spending—the normal running expenses of the great public household—by the means best suited to that purpose: taxes of one sort or another.

There is an even more important explanation for why government as a sector can safely run a deficit. The reason is that the regular income of the public sector comes from taxes, and taxes reflect the general income of the country. Thus most of the money that the government lays out enters the general stream of GDP, where it is largely available to recapture by taxation. The government's "earnings capacity" is therefore far greater than that of any single business. It is comparable only to the immense earning capacity of all businesses put together.

This difference between the limited financial powers of a single firm and the relatively limitless powers of a national government lies at the heart of the basic difference between business and government spending. It helps us understand why the government has a capacity for financial operation that is inherently of a far higher order of magnitude than that of business.

Business firms owe their debts to someone distinct from themselves—someone over whom they have no control—whether this be bondholders or the bank from which they borrowed. Therefore, to service or to pay back its debts, a business must transfer funds from its own possession into the possession of outsiders. If this transfer cannot be made, if a business does not have the funds to pay its bondholders or its bank, it will go bankrupt. If worse comes to worse, they cannot simply print money to pay their debts.

The federal government is in a radically different position. Most of its bondholders, banks, and other people or institutions to who it owes its debts belong to the same community as that whence it extracts its receipts.*

In other words, the government does not have to transfer its funds to an outside group to pay its bonds. It transfers them, mainly, from some members of the national community over which it has legal powers (taxpayers) to other members of the same community (bondholders). The contrast is much the same as that between a family that owes a debt to another family, and a family in which the husband has borrowed money from his wife; or again between a firm that owes money to another, and a firm in which one branch has borrowed money from another. Internal debts do not drain the resources of one community into another, but merely redistribute the claims among members of the same community.

Just the same, some nagging doubts may remain. In view of the fact that our federal debt today figures out to approximately thirteen thousand dollars for every man, woman, and child, it is not surprising that we frequently hear appeals to common sense, telling us how much better we would be without this debt, and how our grandchildren will groan under its weight. Is this true? Suppose we decided that we would pay off the debt. This would mean that our government bonds would be redeemed for cash. To get the necessary cash, we would have to tax ourselves, but what we would really be doing would be transferring money from those of us who are taxpayers to those of us who own government bonds.

A little levity may help. We hear many politicians warn us of the burden of the debt when it falls on the shoulders of future generations. Let us then suppose that the day of reckoning has come and our progeny go to the bank to discover what we have bequeathed them. Breathlessly they open the family safe-deposit box to discover there a bundle of debt, totaling, let us say, twenty-five thousand dollars for each of them. Of course, like all government debt, the burden consists of government bonds. Do you think our progeny will bemoan their fate as they stuff their burden into their suitcases? Or will they stop on the way home to celebrate?

---

*The exception are *foreign* owners of U.S. bonds. We will come back to this later.

THE POWER TO PRINT MONEY

Last, but certainly not least, we must recognize one vast difference between government borrowing and private borrowing. The difference is that all governments possess a power to which no business can ever lay claim. It is the power to create money, a sovereign right of a nation state, like the right to declare war.

Needless to say, this right can lead to disasters when a government rolls the printing presses because it cannot beg, borrow, or tax the funds it needs, usually during wartime. But in normal times, the power to create money also has an extraordinary effect on the creditworthiness of government debt. That is why government bonds normally have lower interest rates than those of the private firms. This is because no one who lends money to a private corporation has the *certainty* of getting it back. In the Great Depression, many major corporations went bankrupt, leaving their bondholders high and dry.

How often has this happened to the bondholders of governments over the two and half centuries of capitalism? The answer is twice—once when the Confederate States of America lost the Civil War, and again when the czarist government of Russia was overthrown in 1917. The reason was the same in both cases—these governments lost their sovereign power to create money. Their bonds, which were formerly "good as gold," were suddenly no better than wallpaper, which is how both of them ended up.

SUMMING UP

After these reassuring words, we need a sobering conclusion. A large and continuing deficit can indeed bring economic troubles in its wake. These are not the troubles of national bankruptcy, however, but the problems of careless national budgeting.

When the federal government undertakes more expenditures than can be paid for by taxes, it must borrow the difference through the issuance of Treasury bonds. Because these bonds are the safest credit instrument available, and because the Treasury will price its bonds at whatever levels are required to sell them, the federal government always has first crack at the nation's savings. All other borrowers—states and localities, businesses, households—have second crack. These borrowers may therefore be crowded out, if the total demand for savings is greater than the supply. Federal government will get the funds it needs, but some of the nonfederal or private borrowers may not get the funds they need.

Even here there is a complication. Suppose we could identify the exact business project that would be crowded out by the last $10 million of government borrowing. There is no doubt that this would cost us the additional wealth and enjoyments that would have flowed from that presumably successful undertaking. Yet, unless we inquire into the use to which the government's borrowing would have been put, we cannot jump to the conclusion that the national interest therefore has been damaged. Suppose the crowded-out private project would have been a luxury apartment complex and the crowding-out government project a slum rehabilitation program. It would not be so easy, in such a case, to declare that crowding out would be a national setback. Maybe it would be a national gain.

The trouble is that there is usually no way of knowing what the "last" dollar of borrowing will be used for in either sector. In times of war we know that the government gets absolute first claim on all resources, including access to savings, and in normal times, especially where there is still too much unemployment, there is a general rule that business ought to have right of way in borrowing. And there are still other times, such as peacetime full employment, when it may be very hard to know which sector ought to be favored in the capital markets. This is all the more the case because we have not yet developed a capital budget for government, as many other nations have.

These considerations by no means touch on all the problems of deficit spending, for example, the complications that may arise if foreigners own a large fraction of the national debt—they own about 25 percent today. The same problem, incidentally, can be applied to the private sector—what happens if foreigners own "too much" of our corporate debt? (We will look into that later.) And there are other questions. What happens if the debt gets so large that interest payments on it seriously strain our tax-raising capacity? This is by no means an imaginary problem for a nation with a very large debt/GDP ratio, such as Italy. Here we might only take note that our own ratio of debt to GDP is very low relative to most other industrial countries, and that our deficit in 1997 was also a smaller fraction of GDP than that of any other capitalist nation.

But our purpose here is not just to reassure our readers with respect to the United States. It is to look at the question of national debts and deficits realistically, shorn of the scare words that prevent us from making informed judgments. Hence a few concluding words to sum up the message of this chapter:

1. *From the economic point of view, the government is a sector, not just a large household.* Unless we understand that vital distinction, we cannot intelligently judge the strengths and weaknesses of government as an economic actor. This can lead to very serious misjudgments, regardless of whether one's political views incline to a smaller, less active government or a larger and more active one.

2. *We cannot determine the size of a deficit accurately unless we recognize that government borrowing is used to pay for investment as well as consumption spending.* That's not always a simple matter to determine. Is government investment strictly a matter of infrastructure, such as roads and bridges? In that case, our 1997 "deficit" would be cut by $70 billion, quite a reduction! Or are education expenditures also a part of investment because, like infrastructure, they are outlays that increase national productivity? Our 1997 government investment comes to $329 billion. If we subtract that amount from total government borrowing, there would be no "deficit" left—in fact, we would have a surplus!

   What we need, in a word, is a plausible estimate of what we wish to count as public investment. That sum—our "capital budget"—would then be properly set against our total borrowing, the remainder being our deficit. That deficit may still be judged too large, which means that government spending should be cut or taxes raised, but we predict that a great deal of the current hysteria would disappear from the deficit question.

   We should note that the Commerce Department is beginning to separate government investment from other government spending. With all its difficulties, a beginning has been made, and the consequences could be substantial in helping us think more clearly about government finance.

3. *Here still remains the need to spend government money intelligently and usefully.* That, too, requires judgment, because spend-

ing that looks wasteful to one person may look sensible to another—compare how differently farm subsidies and airport enlargements appear to farmers and city dwellers respectively. In the end there is no black and white determination of these matters. The moral for all of us is that efficiency and good judgment are just as necessary—and just as hard to find—in the private sector as in the public. Government is part of the economy; the economy is part of government. A little dose of that view might go a long ways to making both sectors run better.

NINE

The Debate About Government

Two big questions still remain concerning the debate about government in the economy. (1) Is it inflationary? (2) Can government add to the growth of GDP? By and large, the conservative side, especially within the business community, answers yes to the first question and no to the second. The liberal side says no—or perhaps maybe—to the first, and yes to the second. Our own views tend to the liberal side, but not entirely so. There is something to be said for both sides of the debate, and we shall try to say it.

First, inflation. Does government spending produce inflation? As we will see, this is a question with question marks: no absolutely clear-cut answer is possible. But we can narrow down the area of disagreement by starting with aspects on which there is unanimity.

Everyone agrees that government spending must be inflationary under certain conditions. These conditions are described by the words "full employment," meaning an economy in which there is only a very small pool of workers available for jobs at going wages, and in which most plant and equipment is being used up to normal capacity. When you have a situation like that, additional government spending is bound to push up prices, either because the added demand for labor will send up wages or because trying to produce more goods than a plant is designed for will send up costs. Thus, no one in his right mind would ever advocate increasing government spending when the economy is already in full boom.

Nevertheless, a few comments have to be made even about this clear-cut case. The first is that full employment is a situation in which additional spending *of any kind* will produce inflation. More household spending or more business spending will bid up wages or send up costs in exactly the same way as more government spending. So it is not the fact that the additional spending originates from the government that is important, but that any kind of increased buying from any sector will bring trouble when we are at full employment.

If we are in such a state and *want* to increase government spending—say, for military preparedness or to launch a program of urban renewal—the only way to avoid inflation is to trim spending in some other sector. In full employment, you cannot have more warfare or more welfare without inflationary consequences unless you make room for the larger government portion of GDP by holding down either household or business buying, or both.

A somewhat less clear-cut case involves the situation at the other end of the economic scale, when the economy is suffering from high levels of unemployment and low levels of utilization. Can you have more government spending under such circumstances without sending up prices? The conventional wisdom of the last several decades was that you could. The presence of millions of idle workers and banks of unused machines make it plausible that you could spend more money, for whatever purpose, without bidding up prices or costs. Perhaps the most convincing illustration was the U.S. experience from 1934 to 1940, when GDP expanded by 50 percent, stimulated by higher government spending, whereas prices rose by less than 5 percent.

This conviction is not so firmly held today as it was in the Depression years. Any economy will be more inflation-prone in good times than in bad—a question we will look into again. So it's not so easy to be sure today that increased government spending, even under conditions of high unemployment and considerable idle plant, might not result in higher prices, along with higher employment and output. On the other hand, the same unhappy conclusion again applies to more spending by business, or from a surge of consumer buying. If we live in an inflation-prone system, *any* increase in demand—not just government—is likely to give inflation a shove.

Here the debate between liberals and conservatives divides on two issues. The first is whether the additional output and employment that government spending may bring forth is worth the additional inflation it may also generate. By and large the liberals say yes, the conservatives, no. These are also questions we will consider again.

The second issue turns on the relative effectiveness of government spending versus private spending in giving us more output. Here the conservatives argue that private spending for plant and equipment increases our capacity to produce, thereby ultimately slowing down inflation because there are more goods to buy. Public spending, on the contrary, it is claimed, adds little or nothing to salable output, and therefore pushes directly on the price level.

There is something to be said for this argument, but not the way it usually is said. When the issue is debated in terms of "public" versus "private" expenditure, we tend to get ideological fervor, not analytical insight. After all, "public" expenditure can be for bombers, which will certainly not increase salable output, or for education, which may indeed increase the output of our labor force. Private output may be concentrated in high technology or in high-rise luxury hotels. Moreover, some kinds of private spending can only be undertaken if they are accompanied, or prepared for, by public spending: we had to build highways before we could build an auto industry, and we may well have to build a public coal port before we can expand the production of coal for export. Thus our own view is that some kinds of expenditure are indeed more inflation-producing than others, but that these kinds are not *necessarily* located in the public sphere. The argument has to be examined in its particulars, not used as a bludgeon.

There is one further aspect to the question of how inflationary government spending is. This centers on the manner in which government spending is financed. Conservatives have no vehement objection to government's borrowing directly from the private sector—for instance, by floating school bonds—or simply by issuing savings bonds. Conservatives may object to the purposes for which the money is spent, but they do not claim that borrowing household or business savings is inflationary. Why should it be more inflationary for New York City to borrow money to renovate its subway system than for Consolidated Edison to borrow money to renovate its power stations?

The inflationary argument is focused on the federal government's borrowing directly from the Federal Reserve banks, by selling them its Treasury securities. This is called monetizing the debt. Monetizing the debt increases the ability of banks to lend money, which, as we shall see in the coming chapter, is the same thing as increasing the amount of money in the system. All economists agree that increasing the amount of money is usually inflationary. The bone of contention is whether money is the chief—or the only—villain. Our own belief is that selling government bonds to finance public spending may help support inflation by making credit more easily available (as we shall see later), but that is by no means the same thing as saying that it is the prime cause of inflation. We will have to be content with that unexplained answer until we go a little further into money and inflation questions up ahead.

DEMAND MANAGEMENT

We turn now to the second major bone of contention—whether government spending can actually increase GDP. Essentially, liberals say yes, conservatives, no. We will present both sides of the case as we see it.

The liberal arguments are already familiar to us because they have been incorporated in our book. They hinge on two matters that should now be very familiar. The first is that government—always meaning local, state, and federal—produces a wide spectrum of outputs, and that these outputs must be examined one by one before general pronouncements can be made about them. When we look at government we see the construction of dams and sewer systems, the support of research, and the creation of soil erosion programs just as much as we see the payments of welfare checks, the proliferation of bureaucracies, and the cost overruns on B-1 bombers. So, of course, we believe that government spending can increase GDP *because it is part of GDP,* and of course we believe that government spending can increase our productivity insofar as it is spending on well-chosen public investment.

Indeed, one of the points of converging opinion between liberals and many conservatives is the growing recognition that government can play an important part in economic growth by shoring up our infrastructure. Infrastructure is a word that covers both old-fashioned public capital, such as dams and waterways and roads and the like—the Panama Canal must be the biggest infrastructure project ever undertaken—and new-fashioned growth-promoting public undertakings, such as research and development and, most important of all, education.

In 1990, economist David Alan Aschauer published a research paper claiming that a decade of neglect and cutting back under the Reagan and Bush administrations had so depleted the nation's stock of public capital that a dollar invested in infrastructure would bring a larger rise in GDP than a dollar spent for private investment.* Greeted originally with widespread skepticism, research has now generally vindicated Aschuaer's position. Government spending on infrastructure fell to only half of what it was in the 1960s, after adjusting for inflation! Unfortunately, the tremendous pressure to cut the deficit during President Clinton's first term stood in the way of repairing this serious problem. Since then a "balanced budget" amendment has been proposed to make all deficits unconstitutional except in special circumstances, such as war, or when a supermajority of Congress votes in favor of a deficit for specified purposes. Over one thousand economists, including nine Nobelists, and the authors of this book, signed a public protest against such an amendment. We will see how it fares.

The second issue is also well rehearsed by now. It is that government can offset gaps in the demand for GDP just as effectively as the business sector, by borrowing savings and spending them. One of the most important conceptual breakthroughs that macroeconomics gives us is a recognition of how the government sector plays a balancing role with respect to the other sectors—borrowing and spending, when the business sector fails to do so, and holding back its spending—actually running a budget surplus—when the private sectors are failing to save enough.

Thus, the liberal side of the argument stresses the role of government as a *demand manager,* taking on the responsibility for creating the volume of demand we need to get up to a satisfactory level of performance. That is not to say that demand managing is an easy objective. There was a time, not so long ago, when liberal economists talked rather glibly of "fine-tuning" the economy, as if we could regulate the level of employment and output with all the precision of a hi-fi set. That easy optimism has long since vanished. We know that it is difficult to bring the economy up to high levels of performance without incurring an unacceptable degree of inflation. We know that we cannot raise or lower taxes or expenditures as if they were just numbers in an equation. The realities of public opinion, political coalitions, or structural resistances in the economy make it utopian to imagine that the government can guide the economy toward some goal like steering a ship in calm

---

*David Alan Aschauer, *Public Investment and Private Sector Growth,* Economic Policy Institute, Washington, D.C., 1990.

weather. The reality is more like trying to keep a compass heading against squalls and rough waves and countercurrents.

Indeed, matters are even worse than we have described. Demand management has not only had to struggle to maintain headway in very rough seas, but it has also been the cause of most modern-day business cycles. No longer can we pin the blame for recession solely on a lagging pace of private investment. To some extent, every recession since World War II can be traced to federal budgetary policies. In 1949, 1954, 1957–1958, and 1960–1961 the government curtailed its military spending without compensating for that curtailment by cutting taxes or raising civilian expenditures. In 1969–1970, 1974–1975, 1980–1982, and again in the first Clinton term government deliberately *created* an economic slowdown through policies aimed at dampening inflation. Inflation was not much affected, but the economy was.

Thus it must be abundantly clear that demand management is no panacea. In its effort to stave off problems, it may create new ones, possibly equally serious. Nonetheless, in the view that we endorse, demand management remains an indispensable tool. This is because we see the economy as inherently subject to booms and busts stemming from the instability of business investment, from waves of optimism and pessimism that affect consumer buying, and from shifts in government policy itself, for instance in the amount of military spending. If we are to avoid the full effect of these shifting winds and currents, we have to use the public sector—increasing its expenditures when the private sector slows down, decreasing them when the private system revs up. Alternatively, we can regulate demand by raising and lowering taxes while keeping public expenditures unchanged. The fact that we have steered badly, sometimes even perversely, does not mean that we should jettison the rudder of federal management. The challenge, rather, is to learn how to use it better.

THE OTHER SIDE OF THE COIN

That's the way liberal-minded economists see it. But another, quite different view, is held by conservative-minded economists, and even more strongly by like-minded political figures. In President Reagan's time it was called "supply side" economics—a phrase meaning that only the private sector was capable of increasing national output on a lasting basis. That term has fallen into disuse. One reason was the often-cited belief that cutting tax rates would impart such an incentive to raise output that government tax revenues would rise even though tax rates were lower. Taxes *were* cut, and output responded favorably, but the growth was nowhere near enough to increase the government's revenues.

In more recent times a new point of view has been advanced strongly by many conservative economists and political spokesmen. It has no single name, but its central theme is that ultimately there is nothing substantial or enduring that government can do to change the autonomous workings of the system—that is, the forces that arise from its spontaneous natural workings. These economists speak of rates of unemployment in a free market as reflecting these autonomous forces of the demand and supply for workers.

The idea of such a normal, internally generated rate of employment seems at first quite convincing. It means that the level of employment at any time will reflect the demand for labor generated by employers across the nation, who can be described as "rational"—that is, intelligent, profit-minded businessmen who want to hire as many workers as their judgment tells them will be profitable. Facing them will be workers who seek work at wages that seem reasonable, given their own best judgment as to the existing and prospective state of things. The ensuing level of employment will represent the best bargain that can be struck between employers and workers, just as any market reconciles the differing interests of buyers and sellers.

One very powerful policy conclusion follows from this reasonable-sounding analysis. It is that the level of employment in a market society reflects as large a body of information as is available in that society. This level of employment may turn out to be too big to be maintained, with the result that wages will fall, or it may be too small, giving rise to labor shortages and wage rises. But that does not invalidate its essential premises: after all, who knows what the "true" state of the economy is at any moment? All that conservatives maintain is that there is no better way of arriving at a sustainable wage rate and its associated level of employment than to let the market do it with as little intervention as possible.

Crucial here is the belief that government can add no information that would result in a higher sustainable level of employment. That is, the men and women who formulate government policies cannot "know" the real market as well as, much less better than, the collective knowledge of its participants, and cannot therefore substitute their judgment for that of the market itself.

The central conservative conclusions follow logically: Government should not try to set minimum wages. It should not take on economic activities not required for the fulfillment of its "legitimate" duties. It should not try to boost demand by "employment-generating" programs that have no roots in the workings of the market itself. Perhaps government spending might improve the existing employment situation, but that would be sheer luck: there is no way of adding to the collective store of information that the market embodies, much less exercising it intelligently and usefully.

This brings us finally to the question we posed at the end of Chapter Seven—is there something we could do about another transformational boom, rather than sitting around and waiting for it to happen? More specifically, in the context of the views we have just examined, is it imaginable that government itself could set into motion such a boom through a program of infrastructural spending—bullet trains and research-and-development assistance to industry, aid to education and reconstruction of the inner cities, and other such public undertakings?

We must be all too familiar with the arguments as to why such a great change could be set into motion by government and why it could not. We have heard enough about why government is much like private investment and why it is not; why it could indeed transform the economic outlook and why it could not.

Then how does one finally make up one's mind about the question? Is it because in the end the arguments of one side seem deeper and more cogent than those of the other? We like to think so. But whether it be for the side that we openly favor or against it, we suspect that another element often plays a crucial role.

Here an anecdote sheds a good deal of light. In *The First New Nation,* sociologist Seymour Martin Lipset contrasts two countries who faced a similar challenge but who responded to it in very different ways. The countries were Canada and the United States, and the common challenge was the presence of a great contiguous wilderness. Out of this common experience emerged two very different folk heroes. For the Canadians it was the scarlet-coated Northwest Mounted Police, bringing national law and order into the newly won wilderness. For the United States it was the cowboy, the embodiment of the individual who made his own law and order. The choice of two such different heroes speaks to the cultural influences and shared visions that influence us powerfully in many social choices, including whether or not we believe in the possibility of a government-led transformational boom. They attest once again, as did our critique of Marx, that economics is not the rock-bottom foundation of the social system. The economy is a vitally important part of society, but all societies ultimately rest on the values, beliefs, and social institutions that different people have developed in their pasts, and that linger on, for better or worse, to influence the ways in which they will create their different futures.

TEN

What Money Is

We are almost done with our first view of macroeconomics, but not quite. We can't really understand how macro flows work until we have understood what is flowing along the streams called consumption and investment. We can call it "income" or "production," but we know it is really something else: It is money. So we will devote two chapters to finding out what money is, so that we can turn from our first view of macro to a first view of micro, the still unexamined aspect of the economy.

Economists like to complain that the single most persistent misconception against which they must do battle is that banks are warehouses stuffed full of money. What *are* they stuffed full of? That is a matter we will spend this chapter investigating.

CASH AND CHECKS

Let us begin by asking, What is money? Coin and currency are certainly money. But are checks money? Are the deposits from which we draw checks money? Are savings accounts money? Government bonds?

The answer is somewhat arbitrary. Basically, money is anything we can use to make purchases with. But there exists a spectrum of financial instruments that serve this purpose—a continuum that varies in liquidity, or the ease with which it can be used for purchasing. By law, coin and currency are money because they are defined as legal tender: a seller must accept them as payment. Checks do not have to be accepted (we have all seen signs in restaurants saying, WE DO NOT ACCEPT CHECKS), although in fact checks are overwhelmingly the most frequent means of payment. Today checks often can be written on savings accounts as well as on checking accounts. On occasion, government bonds are accepted as a means of payment.

Thus, a variety of things can be counted as money. By far the most important general definition is the sum of all cash in the hands of the public plus all checking accounts, which are called demand deposits (because, unlike all savings accounts, they must be paid on demand).

Of these two kinds of money, currency is the form most familiar to us. Yet there is considerable mystery even about currency. Who determines how much currency there is? How is the supply of coins or bills regulated?

We often assume that the supply of currency is set by the government that issues it. Yet when we think about it, the government does not just hand out money, and certainly not coins or bills. When the government pays people, it is nearly always by check.

Then who does fix the amount of currency in circulation? You can answer the question by asking how you yourself determine how much currency you will carry. The answer is that you cash a check when you need more currency than you have, and you put the currency back into your checking account when you have more than you need.

What you do, everyone does. The amount of cash the public holds at any time is no more and no less than the amount that it wants to hold. When it needs more—at Christmas, for instance—the public draws currency by cashing checks on its own checking accounts; when Christmas is past, shopkeepers (who have received the public's currency) return it to their checking accounts.

Thus the amount of currency we have bears an obvious, important relation to the size of our bank accounts, for we can't write checks for cash if our accounts will not cover them.

Does this mean, then, that the banks have as much currency in their vaults as the total of our checking accounts? No, it does not. But to understand that, let us follow the course of some currency that we deposit in our banks for credit to our accounts.

When you put money into a commercial bank, the bank does not hold that money for you as a pile of specially earmarked bills or as a bundle of checks made out to you from some payer. The bank takes notice of your deposit simply by crediting your "account," a computer tape recording your present balance. After the amount of the currency or check has been credited to you, the currency is put away with the bank's general store of vault cash—the cash the teller takes out of the drawer and counts out in front of you—and the checks are sent to the banks from which they came, where they will be charged against the accounts of the people who wrote them.

Thus you might search as hard as you pleased in your bank, but you would find no money that was yours other than a bookkeeping account in your name. This seems like a very unreal form of money, and yet the fact that you can present a check at the teller's window and convert your bookkeeping account into cash proves that your account must be real.

But suppose that you and all the other depositors tried to convert your accounts into cash on the same day. You would then find something shocking. There would not be nearly enough cash in the bank's till to cover the total withdrawals. In 1997, for instance, total demand or other checkable deposits in the United States amounted to a little more than $1 trillion. But the total amount of coin and currency held by the banks was only a third of that.

At first blush, this seems like a highly dangerous state of affairs. But second thoughts are more reassuring. After all, most of us put money into a bank because we do not need it immediately, or because making payments in cash is a nuisance compared with making them by check. Yet there is always the chance—more than that, the certainty—that some depositors will want their money in currency. How much currency will the banks need then? What will be a proper reserve for them to hold?

THE FEDERAL RESERVE SYSTEM

For many years the banks themselves decided what reserve ratio constituted a safe proportion of currency to hold against their demand deposits. Today, however, most large banks are members of the Federal Reserve, a central banking system established in 1913 to strengthen the banking activities of the nation. Under the Federal Reserve System, the nation is divided into twelve districts, each with a Federal Reserve Bank owned by the member banks of its district. In turn, the twelve Reserve Banks are themselves coordinated by a seven-member Federal Reserve Board in Washington. Since the President, with the advice and consent of the Senate, appoints members of the board for fourteen-year terms, they constitute a body that has been purposely established as an independent monetary authority.

One of the most important functions of the Federal Reserve Board is to establish reserve ratios for different categories of banks, within limits set by Congress. Historically these reserve ratios have ranged between 13 and 26 percent of demand deposits for city banks, with a somewhat smaller reserve ratio for country banks. Today, reserve ratios are determined by size of bank and by kind of deposit, and they vary between 18 percent for the largest banks and 8 percent for the smallest. The Federal Reserve Board also sets reserve requirements for time deposits (the technical term for savings deposits). These range from 1 to 6 percent, depending on the ease of withdrawal.

A second vital function performed by the Federal Reserve Banks is that they serve their member banks in exactly the same way as member banks serve the public. Member banks automatically deposit in their Federal Reserve accounts all checks they get from other banks. As a result, banks are constantly clearing their checks with one another through the Federal Reserve System, because their depositors are constantly writing checks payable to someone who banks elsewhere. Meanwhile, the balance that each member bank maintains at the Federal Reserve—its "checking account" there—counts as part of its reserves against deposits, just like the currency in its tills.

Thus we see that our banks operate on what is called a fractional reserve system. That is, a certain specified fraction of all demand deposits must be kept on hand at all times in cash or at the Fed (as economists and bankers call the Federal Reserve). The size of the minimum fraction is determined by the Federal Reserve. It is not determined, as we might be tempted to think, to provide a safe backing for our bank deposits. Under any fractional system, if all depositors decided to draw out their accounts in currency and coin from all banks at the same time, the banks would be unable to meet the demand for cash and would have to close. We call this a run on the banking system. Runs have been terrifying and destructive economic phenomena. Today they no longer pose a dire threat because the Federal Reserve Banks can supply their members with vast amounts of cash, as we shall see.

But why court the risk of runs, however small this risk may be? What is the benefit of a fractional banking system? To answer that, let us look at your bank again.

Suppose its customers have given your bank $1 million in deposits and that the Federal Reserve Board requirements are 20 percent, a simpler figure to work with than the actual one. Then we know that the bank must at all times keep $200,000 either in currency in its own till or in its demand deposit at the Federal Reserve Bank.

But having taken care of that requirement, what does the bank do with the remaining deposits? If it simply lets them sit, either as vault cash or as a deposit at the Federal Reserve, our bank will be very liquid—that is, it will have a great deal of instantly spendable cash—but it will have no way of making an income. Unless it charges a very high fee for its checking services, it will have to go out of business.

And yet there is an obvious way for the bank to make an income while performing a valuable service. The bank can use all the cash and check claims it does not need for its reserve to make loans to businesses or families or to make financial investments in corporate or government bonds. It will thereby not only earn an income, but it will assist the process of business investment and government borrowing.

Thus fractional reserve allows banks to lend or invest part of the funds that have been deposited with them. But that is not their only useful purpose. As we shall see in our next chapter, fractional reserves also give the Fed a means of regulating how much the banking system can lend or invest. In other words, fractional reserves are the lever through which the Federal Reserve authorities can control the quantity of money in the system—namely, the amount of deposits that banks are able to accept.

PAPER MONEY AND GOLD

Our next chapter will take us into the question of how the Fed manages our money. But before we leave the question of what money is, we ought to clear up one last mystery—the mystery of where currency (coin and bills) actually comes from and where it goes. If we examine most of our paper currency, we will find that it has the words "Federal Reserve Note" on it: That is, it is paper money issued by the Federal Reserve System. We understand by now how the public gets these notes: It simply draws them from its checking accounts. When it does so, the commercial banks, finding their supplies of vault cash low, ask their Federal Reserve district banks to ship them as much new cash as they need.

And what does the Federal Reserve Bank do? It takes packets of ones and fives and tens and twenties out of its vaults, where these stacks of printed paper have no monetary significance at all; charges the requisite amount against its member banks' balances; and ships the cash out by armored truck. So long as these new stacks of bills remain in the member banks' possession, they are still not money! But soon they will be passed out to the public, where they will be money. Do not forget, of course, that as a result the public will have that much *less* money left in its checking accounts.

Could this currency-issuing process go on forever? Could the Federal Reserve print as much money as it wanted to? Suppose that the authorities at the Federal Reserve decided to order a trillion dollars worth of bills from the Treasury mints. What would happen when those bills arrived at the Federal Reserve Banks? The answer is that they would simply gather dust in their vaults. There would be no way for the Federal Reserve to "issue" its money unless the public wanted cash. And the amount of cash the public could get is always limited by the amount of money in its checking accounts.

Thus the specter of "rolling the printing presses" has to be looked at knowingly. In a nation such as pre-Hitler Germany, where most individuals were paid in cash, not by check, it was easier to get the actual bills into circulation than it would be in a highly developed check money system such as ours. The roads to inflation are many, but the actual printing of money is not likely to be one of them.*

Are there no limitations on this note-issuing process? Originally there were limitations imposed by Congress, requiring the Federal Reserve to hold gold certificates equal in value to at least 25 percent of all

---

*We have all seen pictures of German workers in the 1920s being paid their wages in wheelbarrow loads of marks. The question is this: why didn't the German authorities simply print paper money with bigger denominations, so that someone who was paid a billion marks a week could get ten 100-million-mark notes, not a thousand 1-million-mark notes? The answer is that it takes time to go through the bureaucratic process of ordering a new print run of higher denomination notes. Imagine a young economist at the finance ministry suggesting to his chief that they ought to stock up on billion-mark notes to be put into circulation six months hence. His superior would certainly be horrified. "You can't do that," he would protest. "Why, an order for billion-mark notes would be— *inflationary!*"

outstanding notes. (Gold certificates are a special kind of paper money issued by the U.S. Treasury and backed 100 percent by gold bullion in Fort Knox.) Soaring inflation rates and the fall in the international value of the dollar in the 1960s gradually resulted in a situation where our gold reserves could not provide the legal backing required by law. Basically there were two ways out. One would have been to change the gold cover requirements from 25 percent to, say, 10 percent. The second way was much simpler: eliminate the gold cover entirely. With very little fuss, this is what Congress did in 1967.

Does the presence or absence of a gold cover make any difference? From the economist's point of view it does not. Gold is a metal with a long and rich history of hypnotic influence, so there is undeniably a psychological usefulness in having gold behind a currency. But unless that currency is 100 percent convertible into gold, any money demands an act of faith on the part of its users. If that faith is destroyed, the money becomes valueless; so long as it is unquestioned, the money is "as good as gold."

Thus the presence or absence of a gold backing for currency is purely a psychological problem, so far as the value of a domestic currency is concerned. But the point is worth pursuing a little further. Suppose our currency were 100 percent convertible into gold—suppose, in fact, that we used only gold coins as currency. Would that improve the operation of our economy?

Recurrently there is a flurry of interest in some kind of gold standard—although not, of course, a reliance on gold coins. But a moment's reflection should reveal that a gold standard would saddle us with a very difficult problem that our present monetary system handles rather easily. This is the problem of how we could increase the supply of money or diminish it, as the needs of the economy changed. With gold coins as money we would either have a frozen stock of money or our supply of money would be at the mercy of our luck in gold mining or the currents of international trade that funneled gold into our hands or took it away. And incidentally, a gold currency would not obviate inflation, as many countries have discovered when the vagaries of international trade or a fortuitous discovery of gold mines increased their holdings of gold faster than their actual output.

How, then, do we explain the worldwide rush to buy gold—a rush that raised the dollar price of gold from thirty-five dollars an ounce—

its official price as late as 1971—to over eight hundred dollars an ounce in 1979, before it fell again to half that level?

Once again, the economist offers no rational explanation for such a phenomenon. There is nothing in gold itself that possesses more value than silver, uranium, land, or labor. Indeed, judged strictly as a source of usable values, gold is rather low on the spectrum of human requirements. The sole reason why people want gold—rich people and poor people, sophisticated people and ignorant ones— is that gold has been for centuries a metal capable of catching and holding our fancy, and in troubled times it is natural enough that we turn to this enduring symbol of wealth as the best bet for preserving our purchasing power in the future. Right or wrong, gold has for centuries been regarded as mankind's most reliable "store of value." Will gold in fact remain valuable forever? And if so, how valuable? There is absolutely no way to answer such a question.

Money is a highly sophisticated and curious invention. At one time or another nearly everything imaginable has served as the magic symbol of money: whales' teeth, shells, feathers, bark, furs, blankets, butter, tobacco, leather, copper, silver, gold, and (in the most advanced nations) pieces of paper with pictures on them, or simply numbers on a computer printout. In fact, anything is usable as money, provided that there is a natural or enforceable scarcity of it so that men can usually come into its possession only through carefully designated ways. Behind all the symbols, however, rests the central requirement of faith. Money serves its indispensable purposes as long as we believe in it. It ceases to function the moment we do not. Money has well been called "the promises men live by."

ELEVEN

How Money Works

Every capitalist nation has a monetary system basically similar to ours. As a consequence, all have developed central banks whose duties are essentially like those of the Federal Reserve—namely, to exert control over the direction and extent of changes in the money supply.

The aim of all central banks is also the same. They want to keep their economies supplied with the "right" amount of money. If money supplies are scarce, the economy will suffer as if it were in a straitjacket—householders and businesses alike seeking in vain for credit from their banks, and householders and businesses alike contracting their economic activity as a result. If money supplies are too large, householders and businesses will find themselves with larger bank accounts than normal, and will be tempted by their liquidity, or by the low interest rates offered by their banks, to increase their spending.

This would seem to make the task of the Federal Reserve rather easy. All it has to do is to take the temperature of the economy and adjust the amount of money accordingly. If the economy is "overheated," with inflation worsening, clearly it is time to cut back on the availability of money. If the economy is in the doldrums, with unemployment rising, just the contrary must be the proper course to follow. It sounds, therefore, as if the job of the central banker is an easy one. As we shall see, it is not.

HOW THE FED WORKS

How does a central banker increase or decrease the supply of money? The key, as we saw in our last chapter, lies in the fact that we have a fractional reserve system in which banks can make loans or investments with "excess" reserves. Excess reserves are simply cash or deposits at the Fed that are greater than those required by law to back up their customers' deposits.

Essentially the Federal Reserve is a system designed to raise or lower the reserve requirements of its member banks. When it raises them, it squeezes its members, who find that they have less free reserves to lend or invest. When the Fed lowers requirements, just the opposite occurs, and member banks are able to lend or invest more of their reserves, thereby making more profit for themselves.

Actually, there are three ways in which the Fed can act. The first is by directly changing the reserve requirements themselves. Because these new reserve requirements affect all banks, changing reserve ratios is a very effective way of freeing or contracting bank credit on a large scale. But because it sweeps across the banking system in an undiscriminating fashion it is used only on rare occasions.

A second means of control uses interest rates as the money-controlling device. Member banks that are short on reserves have a special privilege, if they wish to exercise it. They can borrow reserve balances from the Federal Reserve Bank itself and add them to their regular reserve account at the bank.

The Federal Reserve bank, of course, charges interest for lending reserves; this interest is called the *discount rate.* By raising or lowering this rate, the Federal Reserve can make it attractive or unattractive for member banks to borrow or augment their reserves. Thus, in contrast with changing the reserve ratio itself, changing the discount rate is a mild device that allows each bank to decide for itself whether it wishes to increase its reserves. In addition, changes in the discount rate tend to influence the whole structure of interest rates, either tightening or loosening money. When interest rates are high, we have what we call tight money. This means not only that borrowers have to pay higher rates, but that banks are stricter and more selective in judging the creditworthiness of business applications for loans. Conversely, when interest rates decline, money is called easy, meaning that it is not only cheaper but also easier to borrow.

Although changes in the discount rate can be used as a major means of controlling the money supply and are used to control it in some countries, they are not used for this purpose in the United States. The Federal Reserve Board does not allow banks to borrow whatever they would like at the current discount rate. The discount "window" is a place where a bank can borrow small amounts of money to cover a small deficiency in its reserves, but it is not a place where banks can borrow major amounts of money to expand their lending portfolios. As a result, the discount rate serves more as a signal of what the Federal Reserve would like to see happen than as an active force in determining the total borrowing of banks.

By far the most frequently used is a third technique called open-market operations. This technique permits the Federal Reserve banks to change the supply of reserves by buying or selling U.S. government bonds on the open market.

How does this work? Let us suppose that the Federal Reserve authorities wish to increase the reserves of member banks. They will begin to buy government securities from dealers in the bond market, and they will pay these dealers with Federal Reserve checks.

Notice something about these checks: They are not drawn on any commercial bank! They are drawn on the Federal Reserve Bank itself. The security dealer who sells the bond will, of course, deposit the Federal Reserve's check as if it were any other check, in his or her own commercial bank; and his or her bank will send the Federal Reserve's check through for credit to its own account, as if it were any other check. As a result, the dealer's bank will have gained reserves, although no other commercial bank has lost reserves. On balance, then, the system has more lending and investing capacity than it had before. Thus, by buying government bonds the Federal Reserve has, in fact, deposited money in the accounts of its members, thereby giving them the extra reserves that it set out to create. This is what is meant by *monetizing* the debt.

Conversely, if the monetary authorities decide that member banks' reserves are too large, they will sell securities—the U.S. Treasury notes that make up part of the assets of the Federal Reserve Banks. Now the process works in reverse. Security dealers or other buyers of bonds will send their own checks on their own regular commercial banks to the Federal Reserve in payment for these bonds. This time the Fed will take the checks of its member banks and charge their accounts, thereby reducing their reserves. Since these checks will not find their way to another commercial bank, the system as a whole will have suffered a diminution of its reserves. By selling securities, in other words, the Federal Reserve authorities lower the Federal Reserve accounts of member banks, thereby diminishing their reserves.

Thus we see that there are three ways in which the Federal Reserve can decrease or increase the money supply. It can raise or lower bank reserves. It can raise or lower the discount rate. And it can sell or buy government bonds.

How well do these techniques work? Can the Fed accurately match the supply of money to the country's need for it? Like so many economic issues, the answer is less than crystal clear. There is no doubt that the Fed—or its counterpart central banks abroad—can change the money supply. Whether they can do it accurately, or exactly as they wish, is another question.

Essentially, the Fed faces two different kinds of problems:

1. *It may not know what to do.* This certainly is not meant to impugn the intelligence or economic sophistication of the board of governors of the Federal Reserve System, with its superb technical staff. Rather, it reflects the unhappy condition of "stagflation" that has come to characterize the economy of most Western nations during the last decade or so.

   Stagflation means that the economy is both inflating and stagnating at the same time. Prices may be going up in many industries, although large numbers of men and women cannot find work. This poses a cruel dilemma for the monetary authorities. If they decide that the stagnation aspect of the economy is more serious than the inflationary aspect, they will increase money supplies, but the result may well be an immediate jump in the cost of living and no dramatic improvement in the employment, situation. Contrariwise, if the Fed is more worried about inflation than unemployment, it will reduce the availability of reserves. This may show up quickly in a fall in employment, especially in businesses that depend heavily on bank financing, such as the home construction business, without producing instant relief for price-conscious buyers.

We will be talking about this dilemma again in our next chapters. But we can see it poses a terrible problem for any central bank. Whatever policy it follows—anti-inflation or anti-stagnation—will be painful. Neither will produce quick cures. The danger, then, is that the central bank authorities will vacillate, first easing up on money, then tightening it, then easing up again, then tightening again. It is hardly surprising that the economy does not respond well to such treatment.

2. *It may not be effective in doing what it seeks to do.* Even when the Fed knows clearly what it wishes to do, it cannot always accomplish its aim. The ability of the Fed to control the money supply is often likened to our ability to manipulate a string. It's easy to pull with a string, hard to push with it. So, too, with the Fed. It's easy to tighten money by cutting back on the reserves of member banks in various ways. But it is not so easy to increase the money supply as to reduce it. The Fed may reduce reserve ratios or monetize the debt (buy government bonds on the open market), thereby pumping reserves into the banking system. But it cannot force banks to make loans if they do not wish to do so.

Normally banks *will* wish to, but in bad times—such as the Great Depression—they may prefer to pile up unused reserves than to venture into the risky loan market. If that is the case, there is nothing the Fed can do to get the banks' reserves into the hands of the public.

In addition, the Fed's task is complicated because increases or decreases in the supply of money are not always used to finance or curtail spending for goods and services. They may also be used to add to or to reduce the public's holdings of cash, its liquidity. Suppose, for example, that the officials at the Fed expect an acceleration of inflation and decide to tighten the screws on money to make it more difficult for banks to lend. If things worked out just that way, there would be less lending and therefore less spending, and therefore less pressure on prices in the marketplace. But if the public feels the same way about the future as the Fed, individuals may decide to become less liquid, to spend their money "while it's still good." In that case, the restraining actions of the Fed can be frustrated by a rise in the spending habits of the public.

3. *International developments can limit the Fed's power.* This is a new and important development. Something like an international pool of credit is today available to all industrial nations. A U.S. firm looking for funds can borrow them in Germany or France as easily as from its home bank. And the same is true for firms located abroad. We will have a chance later to look more carefully into this international money market. Here it is enough to recognize that this transnational access to funds greatly limits the power of the Fed, or any central bank, to control long-term interest rates, simply because borrowers can do an end run to other countries' banks.

MONETARISM

This is by no means a complete list of problems facing the Fed. But it is enough to indicate how difficult the art of monetary management must be. Indeed, it is just because the art is so difficult and the outcome of policy so often unexpected that much attention has been drawn in recent years to monetarism, a proposal for a new kind of monetary management suggested a few years ago by the eminent conservative economist and Nobel prizewinner Milton Friedman. Friedman's proposal was simplicity itself. He believed that *nothing* in the system was as important as the quantity of money. Consequently he also believed that the regulation of the money supply should not be left to the judgment of the Federal Reserve authorities. With the best will in the world, he said, they will never get the supply of money right. This is partly because neither they nor anyone else knows the *real* state of the economy at any moment—it takes weeks or months to gather data and interpret it. It is partly because all authorities become "dug into" their previous policy decisions and need a great deal of time to change their minds. It is also because the data may be genuinely ambiguous, capable of justifying more than one direction of monetary management.

The result, in Friedman's view, is that the monetary authorities in all nations more often than not aggravate their countries' plights by expanding the supply of money when they ought to have been reining it in, and vice versa. The right medicine, applied at the wrong time, doesn't cure a disease, it worsens it.

The cure was a bold one. Friedman advocated that the supply of money should be expanded by an unchanging fixed percentage geared to the long-term growth of the nation's output. That way, he asserted, the supply of money would not only accommodate the growing need for larger payrolls and inventories and loans, but the very steadiness of its growth would serve to keep the economy on the track of growth. If we found ourselves headed into a recession, let us say, because of international developments, the steady increase in money supply would add to banks' reserves, encouraging them to expand their loans and thereby to move us out of recession. On the other hand, if we experienced a sudden surge of inflation, the same steady and unchanging rate of growth of bank-lending capability would act as an automatic curb, holding down the banks' ability to finance the inflation-swollen demands of their customers, and thereby serving to mitigate the inflationary pressure.

For a time Friedman's idea had considerable appeal. But it also had its problems. One of them was economic. The problem here was deciding what the regular or normal rate of economic growth is or should be. Friedman's plan was based on the supposition that our capacity to produce goods and services would follow its historical trend, essentially reflecting our long-run increase in productivity. But further examination showed that the increase in productivity was not as automatic as we might once have thought. Furthermore, even if we knew that "natural" forces had propelled the economy forward at about 3 percent a year in the past, could we be sure that that is the appropriate rate of growth for the future? Suppose environmental constraints required us to slow up, or that stubborn unemployment indicated we ought to hurry up? It was not so sure, in other words, that we wanted a steady rate of growth rather than one that fit changing circumstances.

The second problem was political rather than economic. Friedman was effectively asking us to stop monkeying with the system and to let its natural dynamism assert itself. But what if the dynamism wasn't there for a few years? Does this mean that we were prohibited from advancing the economic throttle, even though the economy was losing altitude? If Friedman's plan were followed, that is exactly what we would have had to do, assuring the passengers that the natural aerodynamics of our system would ultimately give us a smoother and safer flight than the one we'd get by allowing the pilot to override the automatic flight-control machinery.

That was probably the fatal flaw in Friedman's plan. It mirrors our skepticism regarding "hands-off" economics. Right or wrong, the trend over the last century has been in the direction of increasing our intervention into the workings of the system. This is not only because many economists believe that we *can* intervene effectively, despite all the problems raised by Friedman and his fellow monetarists, but also because there has been a growing political pressure to "do something" about bad economic performance. The willingness to stand by and allow the system to work out its own destiny is largely a thing of the past. The philosophy of Adam Smith has been pushed aside by that of John Maynard Keynes. We may not be able to intervene very effectively; we may indeed bring about outcomes that are different from those we anticipated. In a word, Milton Friedman's warnings may be borne out in fact. But it seems unrealistic that we will content ourselves ever again with a passive attitude toward the economic system. "Doing nothing" sounds like a feasible policy option, but in fact it is not.

III

MICROECONOMICS—
THE ANATOMY OF
THE MARKET SYSTEM

TWELVE

How Markets Work

It seems crazy that economics should come in two "parts"—microeconomics and macroeconomics. And it is a little crazy, for there is only one economy. Yet it is a fact that certain kinds of problems, such as those we have been looking into, reveal themselves most clearly from a macro perspective that stresses the large flows of total saving and investment and government spending, but that the same macro perspective sheds very little light on other types of economic activity, especially those having to do with the kinds of output we produce. These questions about the choices we make as producers or consumers—questions that have immense consequences for our economic life—require a different vantage point, one that highlights the activities of buyers and sellers, of consumers and businessmen. This is the vantage point of the marketplace—the grocery store, the wheat pit, the buying office—where the interaction of buyers and sellers provides the flesh-and-blood encounters we lose sight of in studying GDP.

THE PRICE SYSTEM

The micro point of view brings us immediately to look into the question of prices, a question we have ignored entirely except insofar as we talked about the level of prices when we looked into inflation. But microeconomics wants to explain how particular individual prices are determined in the arena called the marketplace. Hence, microeconomics begins with a study of supply and demand, the words we hear and use all the time, without a very clear idea of what they mean.

Often we speak of supply and demand as if the phrase meant some general law of economic life such as the "law" that "what goes up must come down." But there is no such law, and if there were, it would not be the law of supply and demand. Instead, supply and demand is a way of understanding how the clash (competition) of buyers and sellers in the marketplace brings about prices that "clear" the market—a word we will immediately investigate—or why the clash sometimes fails to bring about such prices. *Supply and demand, in other words, inform us about how markets generate a kind of order in the system,* keeping the different actors in the economy together in ways we caught a glimpse of in Chapter Two when we looked at Adam Smith's conception of the economic world.

So we shall begin by clarifying what we mean when we speak about demand. Most people think the word just means a certain volume of spending, as when we say that the demand for automobiles has fallen off or the demand for gold is high. But that is not what the economist has in mind when he defines demand as part of his explanation of markets. Demand means not just how much we are spending for a given item, but how much we are spending for that item *at its price,* and how much we would spend *if its price changed.*

Furthermore, economists make an important generalization about the behavior of our buying in the face of changing prices. It is that we tend to buy less when prices rise and more when they fall. This sounds like an awfully simple generalization, but as we shall see, a great deal can be built on it. There are two reasons why economists believe it to be true. First, as prices fall we are *able* to buy more, because our incomes stretch further. Second, as prices fall we are *willing* to buy more because at its cheaper price the commodity looks more attractive compared with other commodities.*

---

*We can easily understand why our ability to buy will increase as prices fall, but why our willingness? The answer lies in what economists call the "utility," or pleasure, we get from most goods. Generally, as we add more and more units of one good during a given period, the addition of our pleasure diminishes. One steak dinner in the week is wonderful; two are fine; three okay; seven a bore. These diminishing increments of pleasure are called diminishing marginal utility. Because each successive steak dinner brings less pleasure, we are willing to buy more of them only if their price falls. We may be willing to pay a lot for the first (and only) steak dinner of the week, but we will certainly not pay much for the seventh one.

From this plausible reasoning, economists construct a widely used and very helpful representation of our market behavior, called a *demand curve.* The diagram following shows such a curve. Let's suppose it is designed to show how many shirts will be bought in a department store over a period of a week at different prices. If we look at the dotted lines on the graph, we can see that this (imaginary) example shows that if shirts are priced at fifty dollars, only fifty will be bought. If they are priced at twenty-five dollars, one hundred will be bought. If they are reduced to ten dollars, two hundred will be bought.

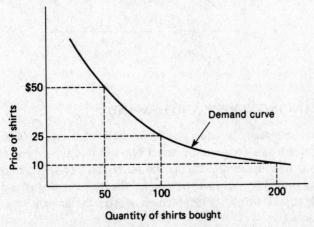

Now what about supply? As we would expect, sellers also react to price changes, but in exactly the opposite direction from buyers. The higher the price, the more sellers are able and willing to put on the market; the lower the price, the less. Sellers are after all presumed to be profit maximizers and there are larger profits to be earned when prices are high. We're not talking about whether a manufacturer might not be able to produce more cheaply at high volumes. The question, rather, is whether General Motors or the local farmer will be willing and able to offer more output to buyers *right now,* with their existing land and equipment, if the price is high rather than low. The answer is obviously yes.

Therefore we can depict a normal supply curve as rising, instead of falling the way a demand curve does. How steeply it rises depends on how much a supplier can bring to market quickly if the price goes up. A farmer may be stuck with a given crop. General Motors may be able to jam a lot of cars through by running three shifts. Here is what a typical short-run supply curve might look like:

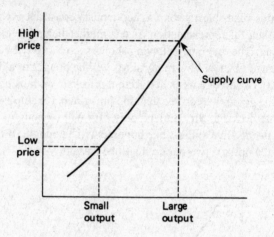

BALANCING SUPPLY AND DEMAND

We are now ready to understand how the market mechanism works. Undoubtedly you've seen the point. The fact that supply and demand behaviors are different and opposite for buyers and sellers allows the system to find a price that will "clear" the market—that is, a price at which buyers will want to purchase exactly the amount that sellers want to sell.

The best way to grasp the supply-and-demand mechanism is to run an imaginary example in our heads. Suppose that a store is selling blouses at $29.95. It has an inventory of a hundred dozen blouses, and it expects to sell its stock out in a month. The buyer reports that the blouses "won't move." What she means is that the demand for blouses at $29.95 isn't enough to get the merchandise into customers' hands. Since the store cuts its losses by getting rid of the blouses it has bought already, the buyer cuts the price of blouses to $10.95 to reduce inventories and possible losses. Now the blouses start to sell. In fact, they go so fast that the buyer tries to reorder, but at much lower prices than before, so that she can continue to price them at $10.95 and still make a profit. What she finds, however, is that the manufacturer can't fill her orders at the lower price she wants. There is a lot of demand for cheap blouses, but no supply.

The question is: Is there a price that will make both the supplier and the customer happy? The answer is yes—the price that will equate the quantity of blouses demanded to the quantity supplied. We can see that in the next graph, below, where the "equilibrium" price is $19.95.

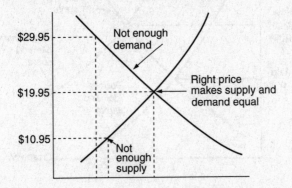

The point is not to get too hung up on the curves, which can be drawn in all sorts of shapes. It is to remember that the curves represent the differing ways we behave as buyers and sellers; and the point of the diagrams, with their crossing curves, is to make clear that as prices change, these differing behaviors can be made mutually compatible, a remarkable fact, when you think about it.

What we have learned so far is that markets, left to themselves, will arrive at an equilibrium price at which they will clear. But markets are rarely, if ever, left to themselves. Buyers and sellers are constantly changing their tastes or experiencing changes in their incomes and costs. As a result, they will bid for more goods at the old price, or will not be willing to buy as much as before. Sellers, too, find themselves willing and able to supply larger or smaller quantities to the market at each price. No supplier or demander actually knows the shapes of the neat supply and demand curves that we so easily draw. What then?

The answer, of course, is that prices change. When we are willing and able to buy more, we say that demand rises, and everyone knows that the effect of rising demand is to lift prices. We can see this in the first simple graph following. The solid lines show supply and demand and equilibrium price *before* some change—say, higher incomes—has boosted demand. The dashed line shows what happens to demand when incomes rise, and what happens to price as a result. It goes up. Of course the mechanism also works in reverse. If incomes fall, so does demand—and so does price.

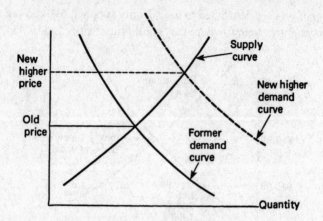

Just to round the thing out, we can also show in a graph what happens when sellers are less willing to supply goods at the same quantities, perhaps due to a rise in costs. When supply decreases, prices rise, as the second figure following makes plain. If supply increases, prices fall, as we can also see.

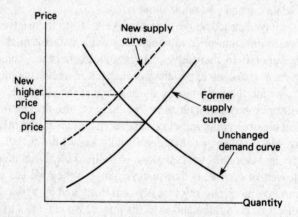

THE MARKET AS A RATIONING SYSTEM

Now look at what this shows us. All the buyers and sellers who can afford and are willing to pay the equilibrium price (or more) will get the goods they want. All those who cannot, will not. So, too, all the sellers who are willing and able to supply the commodity at its equilibrium price or less will be able to consummate sales. All those who cannot will not.

Thus the market, in establishing an equilibrium price, has in effect allocated the goods to some buyers and withheld it from others. It has permitted some sellers to do business and denied that privilege to others. Note that the market is, in this way, a means of excluding certain people from economic activity, namely customers with too little money or with too weak desires, or suppliers unwilling or unable to operate at a certain price. It is, in fact, a rationing mechanism!

Our view of the price system as a rationing mechanism helps to clarify the meaning of two words we often hear as a result of intervention into the market-rationing process: shortage and surplus.

In everyday language we often say that there is a shortage of housing for low-income groups—meaning that poor people cannot find housing that they can afford. Yet as we have seen in every market there are always some buyers who are unsatisfied. We have previously noted, for instance, that in our market for blouses, all buyers who could not or would not pay $19.95 had to go without. Does this mean there was a shortage? In economic terminology, no. A shortage in economic terminology does not mean there are no unsatisfied people in a market. It means only that no one who is willing and able to meet the going price is unable to get the goods he or she wants.

In a market that "clears," no such buyers exist. To be sure, there may be many would-be buyers happy to buy blouses at, say, $16.95, but there are none for sale at that price. Thus "shortage" only refers to buyers who are willing and able to pay the going price *but who cannot get their demands filled at that price.*

Why not? The answer must be that some nonmarket agency—in medieval times, perhaps the Church; in our day, more likely some government agency—has set the price below the equilibrium level. Now buyers who could not get blouses at $16.95 come crowding into the store—only to find that there are not enough blouses to meet the swollen demand. Who will go without—the buyers who were willing and able to pay the higher price, or the new "lucky" buyers who are now able to pay the lower price? The answer is queues in stores to buy things before they are gone, under-the-counter deals to get on a preferred list, or black or gray markets selling goods illegally at higher prices than are officially sanctioned.

The opposite takes place with a surplus. Suppose the government sets a price floor above the equilibrium price, for instance, when it supports the price of corn above its free-market price. In this situation, the quantity supplied is greater than that demanded. In a free market, the price would fall until the two quantities were equal. But if the government continues to support the commodity, then the quantity bought by private industries does not have to be as large as the quantity offered by farmers. Unsold amounts—the surplus—will be bought by government.

Thus the words "shortage" and "surplus" mean situations in which sellers and buyers remain active and unsatisfied *because the price mechanism has not eliminated them from the marketplace.* This is very different from a free market where buyers and sellers who cannot meet the going price are not taken into account. Most people, who have no demand for fresh caviar at eighty dollars per tin, do not complain of a caviar shortage. If the price of fresh caviar were set by government decree at one dollar a pound, there would soon be a colossal shortage.

What about the situation with low-cost housing? Essentially what we mean when we talk of a shortage of inexpensive housing is that we view the outcome of this particular market situation with noneconomic eyes and pronounce the result distasteful. By the standards of the market, the poor who cannot afford to buy housing are only one more example of the rationing process that takes place in every market. When we single out certain goods or services (such as a doctor's care) as being in "short supply," we imply that we do not approve of the price mechanism as the appropriate means of allocating scarce resources in these particular instances. Our disapproval does not imply that the market is not as efficient a distributor as ever. What we do not like is the outcome of the market-rationing process. In other words, for all its worth, efficiency is not the only criterion by which we judge the market system.

That word efficiency brings us to the last and perhaps most important aspect of how markets work. This is the ability of markets to allocate goods and services more effectively than other systems of rationing, particularly planning in one form or another.

There is no question that the market is one of the most extraordinary social inventions in human history. If we recall the attributes of the pre-market societies of antiquity we may remember that they typically suffered from two difficulties. If they were run mainly by tradition, they tended to be inert, passive, changeless. It's very hard to get things done in a traditional economy if anything has to be done in a new way—if, for instance, a change in climate forces a search for new ways of growing food or catching game.

A command system, ancient or modern, has a different inherent problem. It is good in undertaking big projects but not in running a complex system. In addition, the presence of political power in the economic mechanism, either as a large bureaucracy or as an authority capable of sticking its nose into daily life, becomes an endless source of inefficiency and irritation.

Against these two difficulties, the price system has two great advantages: it is highly dynamic, and it is self-enforcing. That is, on the one hand it provides an easy avenue for change to enter the system, as imaginative or ambitious individuals try new approaches or invent new goods. In addition, it allows these individuals to get a fair trial without first getting anyone's official permission: all you have to do is to sell your product!

The second (self-enforcing) attribute of the market is especially useful with regard to the rationing function. In place of ration tickets, with their almost inevitable black markets or cumbersome inspectorates or queues of customers trying to be first in line, the price system operates without any kind of visible administrative apparatus or side effects. The energies that must go into planning, or the frictions that come out of it, are alike rendered unnecessary by this remarkable self-policing mechanism. With all its difficulties, which we have by no means fully enumerated or examined, it is this capacity for self-adjustment and self-correction that sets economics apart from—although by no means above—its sister social disciplines.

That always comes as a surprise. We think of rationing as a formal, inflexible way of sharing goods—one ticket, one loaf of bread. This seems just the opposite of the free, unimpeded flux of marketplace. And in some ways it is indeed as different as can be. Just the same, the price mechanism performs a rationing function, exactly as do ration tickets. Money can be thought of as a system of flexible ration coupons. Indeed, there is nothing more important to grasp than this central purpose that markets serve. They are simply sophisticated rationing mechanisms.

On the other hand, the system has the defects of its virtues. If it is efficient and dynamic, it is also devoid of values. It recognizes no valid claim to the goods and services of society except those of wealth and income. Those with incomes and wealth are entitled to the goods and services that the economy produces; those without income and wealth receive nothing.

This blindness of the market to any claim on society's output except wealth or income creates very serious problems. It means that those who inherit large incomes are entitled to large shares of output, even though they may have produced nothing themselves. It means that individuals who have no wealth and who cannot produce—perhaps simply because they cannot find work—have no way of gaining an income through the economic mechanism. To abide just by the market system of distribution, we would have to be willing to tolerate individuals starving on the street.

Therefore, every market society interferes to some extent with the outcome of the price-rationing system. It does so when an "economic problem" crosses the line to become a "social problem." In times of military emergency the nation issues special permits that take precedence over money and thereby prevents the richer members of society from buying up all the supplies of scarce and costly items. In depressed areas, it may distribute basic food or clothing to those who have no money to buy them. Historically speaking, it has used taxes and transfers to an ever-increasing extent to replace the ration tickets of money in accordance with the prevailing sense of justice, rather than by the standards of efficiency. It is, in fact, in the tension between the claims of efficiency and those of justice that much of the division between conservative and liberal points of view is to be found.

THIRTEEN

Where Markets Fail

Up to this point we have been concerned with how markets work. Now we must look into some situations where they don't. One of these has to do with instances where marketers lack information and have no way of making intelligent decisions and where, therefore, the results of the market will reflect ignorance, luck, or accident rather than informed behavior. A second case involves what are known as "pure public goods"—goods whose intrinsic characteristics mean that they cannot be allocated efficiently by private markets. Closely related in a third category of goods whose purchase, or failure to purchase, affects third parties' welfares and not just those of buyers or sellers. Market economies also need some social investments with longer payback periods than private markets are prepared to endure. Finally, there are some goods, health care being an example, which the public simply wants to see more equally distributed than goods and services in general. We'll take these up, one at a time.

THE PREVALENCE OF IGNORANCE

The whole market system is built on the assumption that individuals are *rational* as well as acquisitive—that marketers will have at least roughly accurate information about the market. A good example of the importance of information is the situation faced by the tourist in a bazaar of a country where he or she doesn't know a word of the language. Such a buyer has no way of knowing what the price of an article ought to be. That's why tourists so often return triumphantly with their bazaar trophies—only to discover that the same items were for sale in their hotel at half the price.

Without correct or adequate information marketers obviously cannot make correct decisions. But typically many marketers do *not* have adequate information. Consumers guide themselves by hearsay, by casual information picked up by random sampling, or by their susceptibility to advertising. Who has time to investigate which brand of toothpaste is really best or even tastes best? Even professional buyers, such as industrial purchasing agents, cannot know every price of every product, including all substitutes.

The lack of information can be remedied, at least up to a point, but the remedy costs money or its equivalent—time. Few of us have the resources or patience to do a complete research job on every item we buy, nor would it even be necessarily rational to do so. Thus a certain amount of ignorance always remains in all markets, causing prices and quantities to differ from what they would be if we had complete information. These differences can be very great, as anyone knows who has ever discovered, with sinking heart, that he or she paid "much too much" for a given article or sold it for "much too little."

Another important cause of market failure lies in the destabilizing effect of "perverse" expectations. Suppose that a rise in prices sets off rumors that prices will rise still more. This is common experience in inflationary times, when the mounting prices of goods leads us to expect that prices will be still higher tomorrow. In this case, we do not act as ordinary demanders, curtailing our purchases as prices go up. Instead, we all rush in, with the result that prices go higher still. Meanwhile, sellers, seeing prices go up, may decide not to take advantage of good times by increasing their offerings, but to hold back, waiting for tomorrow's even higher prices. Thus demand goes up and supply goes down—a recipe for skyrocketing market prices.

Such perverse price movements can lead to very dangerous consequences. They play a major role in the cumulative, self-sustaining processes of inflation or collapse. They can cause commodity prices to shoot to dizzying heights or plummet to the depths. At its worst, perverse behavior threatens to make an entire economy go out of control, as in the case of hyperinflations or panics. At best, it disrupts smooth orderly markets and brings shocks and dislocations to the economy.

Can these market failures be remedied? Some can; some cannot. Ignorance can certainly be reduced by better economic reporting or by truth-in-advertising laws. Perverse behavior can be lessened by persuasive pronouncements from important public figures.

But we must recognize that there is a residue of arbitrariness even in the best-intentioned remedies. Take the matter of consumer information. We "inform" the consumer, through labels on cigarette packages, that smoking is dangerous, but we do not prohibit the advertising of cigarettes. We spread market information by having the incomprehensible contents of medications printed on their containers, but we allow the consumer to be misinformed through advertising that claims superiority of one kind of aspirin over another.

Why? There is no clear rationale in these cases. Essentially we are trying to repair omissions in the market system—injecting information so that consumers can make better choices—without becoming paternalistic. Perhaps we think more mistakes would be made by a government trying to prevent individuals from making mistakes than individuals would themselves make. Or perhaps we just don't want the large governments that would be necessary to prevent individual mistakes.

That is perhaps as it should be. But the consequence is that the market will continue to produce less than wholly satisfactory or efficient results because a residue of ignorance or misinformation is allowed to remain—or remains despite our best efforts.

PURE PUBLIC GOODS

Now we must turn to the range of problems that derive from the fact that certain kinds of output in our system do not have the characteristics of the ordinary goods or services that allow them to be sold in private markets. We call such outputs *pure public goods.* Since pure public goods are not easy to define, let us start by illustrating the properties of goods such as defense, the national weather service, or lighthouses. Such goods have three peculiar characteristics:

First, the consumption of a public good by any one individual does not interfere with its consumption by another. A lighthouse is as effective for ten boats as for one. A weather service is as useful for one hundred million TV viewers as for one hundred. By way of contrast, private goods—the food, clothing, or doctors' services that we use—cannot also be consumed by you.

Second, no one can be excluded from the use of a public good. We can deny you the use of your cars. But there is no way of denying you the use of our national defense system.

Last, with normal goods our private consumption depends on our individual decisions to spend or not spend our incomes. But there is no way that we can, by ourselves, buy defense, weather services, or a lighthouse service.* We must agree how much to buy!

As a result of these three characteristics there is no way to set up a market where citizens will be willing to pay voluntarily for national defense even though everyone values it.

ANOTHER REASON WHY ECONOMISTS DISAGREE

Markets "clear," equating supply and demand, without the bureaucratic problems of nonmarket allocations. No one disagrees with that. *But how long will they take to clear? How much political and social disarray will they create in the process of clearing?* There is lots of room to disagree about that. It is in fact another of the reasons that economists often fail to see eye-to-eye about things.

By and large, conservative economists stress the speed of market clearing and minimize the negative side effects that a market's dynamism creates. Liberals often look at the other side of the same coin. They see markets that adjust slowly with a lot of adverse income effects during the adjustment process. For example, think of U.S. government agricultural price supports for commodities such as corn. If subsidies were to be eliminated quickly, per bushel prices would plunge, driving a lot of inefficient farmers out of business. In the end farming would become more efficient, but during the transition a lot of farm families would be thrown off their farms and be forced to find alternative sources of employment at lower wages than what they had been earning in farming. Many rural communities would disappear and others would become much smaller.

In this case the divisions in opinion tend not to be those between liberal and conservative economists but between economists who live in farm states and those who don't. Which side is right? The answer is not

---

*Not even if we were immensely rich or absolute monarchs? In that case we would not have a market system, but a command economy catering to one person. Then indeed there would be no distinction between public and private goods.

merely one of establishing (if we could) a timetable for market movements or a count of the persons affected by its movement. It is also a
matter of the importance we attach to the benefits of those whom a free
market assists, versus the costs to those who are shouldered aside.
What value does one place on the family farm? There is no "right" answer to these questions, and that is why economists will continue to
disagree about such things as agricultural subsidies.

EXTERNALITIES

Our third source of market failure is closely connected with the attributes of public goods. It is the problem of allowing for what economists
call the *externalities* of production; that is, for the effects of the output
of private goods and services on persons other than those who are directly buying or selling or using the goods in question.

The standard example of an externality is the smoke from the local
factory. The smoke imposes medical bills and cleaning bills on households that may not use any of the factory's output. Or take the noise
near a jetport. That damages the eardrums—and lowers the real estate
values—of individuals who may never benefit from the propinquity of
the airport, indeed who may never fly.

Externalities bring us to one of the most vexing and sometimes dangerous problems in our economic system—controlling pollution.

What is pollution, from an economic point of view? It is the production of wastes, dirt, noise, congestion, and other things we do not want.
Although we don't think of smoke, smog, traffic din, and traffic jams as
part of society's production, these facts of economic life are certainly
the consequences of producing things we do want. Smoke is a part
of the output process that also gives us steel or cement. Smog arises
from the production of industrial energy and heat, among other things.
Traffic is a by-product of transportation. In current jargon, economists
call these unwanted by-products "bads," to stress their relation to
things we call "goods."

The basic reason that externalities exist is technological: we do not
know how to produce many goods cleanly, i.e., without wastes and
noxious by-products. But there is also an economic aspect to the problem. Even when we do know how to produce cleanly, externalities can
exist because it is cheaper to pour wastes into a river than to alter the
manufacturing process to eliminate waste. That is, it is cheaper for the

individual or the firm, but it may not be cheaper for the community. A firm may dump its wastes in a river "for free," but people living downstream will suffer the costs of having to cope with polluted water. Yet the people buying paper, not living in the communities affected by paper production, are only interested in buying cheap paper. They will not voluntarily buy clean (expensive) paper.

Finally, we should note that some externalities are not "bads," but "goods." A new office building may increase the property value of a neighborhood. Here is a *positive* externality. The benefit gained by others results from the new building but is not paid to the owners of that building. Such externalities give some private goods the partial attributes of public goods.

Faced with the ugly view of smoke belching from a factory chimney, sludge pouring from a mill into a lake, automobiles choking a city, or persons being injured by contaminants, most ecologically concerned persons cry for regulation: "Pass a law to forbid smoky chimneys or sulfurous coal. Pass a law to make mills dispose of their wastes elsewhere or purify them. Pass a law against automobiles in the central city."

What are the economic effects of regulation? Essentially, the idea behind passing laws is to internalize a previous externality. That is, a regulation seeks to impose a cost on an activity that was previously free for the individual or firm—although not free, as we have seen, for society. This means that individuals or firms must stop the polluting activity entirely or bear the cost of whatever penalty is imposed by law, or else find ways of carrying out their activities without giving rise to pollution.

Is regulation a good way to reduce pollution? Let us take the case of a firm that pollutes the environment in the course of producing goods or services. Suppose a regulation is passed, enjoining that firm to install antipollution devices—smoke scrubbers or waste treatment facilities. Who bears this cost?

The answer seems obvious at first look: The firm must bear it. But if the firm passes its higher costs along in higher selling prices, we arrive at a different answer. Now a little economic analysis will show us that the cost is in fact borne by three groups, not just the firm. First, the firm will bear some of the cost because at the higher price, it will sell less output. How much less depends on the price sensitivity of demand for its product. But unless demand is totally insensitive, its sales and income must contract.

Two other groups also bear part of the cost. One group is the factors of production—labor and the owners of physical resources. Fewer factors will be employed because output has fallen. Their loss of income is therefore also a part of the economic cost of antipollution regulation. Last, of course, is the consumer. Prices will rise so that the consumer must also bear some share of the cost of regulation.

Offsetting all these costs is the fact that each of these three groups and the general public now have a better environment. There is no reason, however, why each of these three groups, singly or collectively, should think that its benefit outweighs its cost. Most of the benefit is likely to go to the general public, rather than to the individuals actually involved in the production or consumption of the polluting good or service.

Thus a regulation forcing car manufacturers to make cleaner engines will cost the manufacturers some lost sales, will cost the consumer added expense for a car, and will reduce the income going to land, labor, and capital no longer employed making engines. As part of the public, all three groups will benefit from cleaner air, but each is likely to feel its specific loss more keenly than its general gain.

Is regulation useful? Case by case, it's often hard to say. That is why economists tend to apply a general rule: Regulations are good or bad, *mainly depending on their ease of enforcement.* Compare the effectiveness of speed limits, which attempt to lessen the externality of accidents, and of regulations against littering. It is difficult enough to enforce speed laws, but it is almost impossible to enforce antilittering laws. On the other hand, regulation of the disposal of radioactive wastes is simpler to enforce because the polluters are few and easily supervised.

This in turn is largely a matter of cost. If we were prepared to have traffic policemen posted on every mile of highway or every city block, regulation could be just as effective for speed violations or littering as for radioactive waste disposal. Obviously the cost would be horrendous, and so would most people's reactions to being overpoliced.

A second way to cope with pollution is to tax it. When a government decides to tax pollution (often called effluent charges), it is essentially creating a price system for disposal processes. If an individual company found that it could clean up its own pollutants more cheaply than paying the tax, it would do so, thereby avoiding the tax. If the company could not clean up its own pollutants more cheaply than the tax cost, which is often the case, it would pay the necessary tax and look to the state to clean up the environment.

The effluent charge looks like, but is not, a license to pollute. It is a license that allows you to produce some pollutants for a price. Prices could be set to make all pollution prohibitively expensive but are usually set to allow some pollution since the environment has some "free" self-cleaning capacity.

As a result of effluent charges, an activity that was formerly costless is no longer so. Thus, in terms of their economic impacts, these charges are just like government regulations. In fact, they are a type of government regulation. The difference is that each producer can decide whether it pays to install clean-up equipment and not pay the tax, or to pollute and pay whatever tax costs are imposed.

Which is better, regulation or taxation? Practical considerations are likely to decide. For example, taxation on effluents discharged into streams is likely to be more practical than taxation on smoke coming from chimneys. The state can install a sewage treatment plant, but it cannot clean up air that is contaminated by producers who find it cheaper to pay a pollution tax than to install smoke-suppressing equipment. Moreover, to be effective, a pollution tax should vary with the amount of pollution; a paper mill or a utility plant would pay more taxes if it increased its output of waste or smoke. One of the problems with taxation is that of installing monitoring equipment. It is difficult to make accurate measurements of pollution or to allow for differences in environmental harm caused by the same amount of smoke or noxious gasses or just plain heat coming from two factories located in different areas.

The third way of dealing with pollution is to subsidize polluters to stop polluting. In this case the government actually pays the offending parties to clean up the damage they have caused or to stop causing it. For example, a township might lessen the taxes on a firm that agreed to install filters on its stacks. This is, of course, paying the firm to stop polluting.

There are cases when subsidies may be the easiest way to avoid pollution. For example, it might be more effective to pay homeowners to turn in old cans and bottles than to try to regulate their garbage-disposal habits or to tax them for each bottle or can thrown away. Subsidies may therefore sometimes be expedient means of achieving a desired end, even if they may not be the most desirable means from other points of view.

LENGTHENING TIME HORIZONS

Now consider another instance of market failure far removed from those we have mentioned. It has to do with the time horizon that can be rationally applied to market processes—if by "rational" we mean profitable. In a word, will markets provide a setting in which very long-term, very risky, but potentially invaluable research and development take place?

Consider what are probably the two hottest private industries in America today—biotechnology firms and the new telecommunications Internet firms. How did these two industries come into existence?

In the early 1960s the federal National Institutes of Health started spending several billion dollars per year on research and development in what was then called biophysics. Seminal breakthroughs followed—the double helix, DNA, recombinant DNA, etc. Twenty-five to thirty years later a big important profitable private industry with tens of billions of dollars in sales came into existence. But no private firm using normal private decision-making rules would ever have made these original investments. Risks were too high and the time lags until profits could be made were too long. Using discounted net present values (the normal market mechanism for evaluating the value of future returns) today's market value of a dollar that will not be received until ten years from now is approximately zero.

The Internet started twenty-five years ago as a nuclear-bomb-proof communications system; thereafter as a National Science Foundation project; and only recently as a field where firms can make a lot of money. That last would not have happened without social investments made with time horizons far beyond those of private firms.

Or consider education. No hard-nosed capitalistic mother or father would ever invest in sixteen years of education for their children. Sixteen years of money in with no money out—the payoffs are too uncertain and too far into the future. No society has ever become literate solely based upon private education. Yet nothing pays off economically for a society more than having an educated work force.

As a result, investments in education, infrastructure, and research and development have to be at least partly financed by governments. Markets underprovide them.

The trouble is that markets distribute goods and services in accordance with the distribution of income and wealth. Those with money get; those without money do not get. For many products, distributions based upon market incomes yield acceptable social outcomes. But there are some products, such as health care, where we, as a society, have far more egalitarian preferences. We aren't willing to see ourselves, or others, go without health care simply because we do not have enough money to pay for health care—the market result. As a result governments interfere with the market, helping to pay for health care for the elderly (Medicare); and fully paying for it with the poor (Medicaid). Subsidized private health insurance helps those in-between with special tax breaks.

PUBLIC EXPENDITURES

When private markets don't work, the usual remedy is government. How do we then determine the level of provision of such publicly provided goods? We eschew the market mechanism and avail ourselves of another means of decisionmaking: voting. We vote for the amount of public expenditures we want; and because voting is a curious mechanism, sometimes we oversupply ourselves with these goods and sometimes we undersupply ourselves. One of the reasons that voting is a curious mechanism is that there is no way of doling it out in small pieces, the way we spend our income. Our vote is Yes or No. As a result, we may swim in health care and starve in education because health care has "friends in Congress" and education does not.

Is there a remedy for the problem? Some economists have suggested that we should try to bring as many public goods as possible into the market system by getting rid of their public characteristics. We could charge admission to the city's parks, so that we could produce only as much park service as people were willing to buy. We could charge tolls on all roads, even streets, and limit the building or repair of highways to the amount of private demand for road services. We might limit the use of law courts to those who would hire the judge and jury. Public policemen could be replaced with private policemen who would only protect those who wear a badge attesting to their contribution to the police fund.

Such a privatization of public goods might indeed bring the level of their production up, or down, to the amount that we would consume if they were strictly private goods, like cars or movie tickets. The problems are twofold. First, there are often technical difficulties in making many public goods into private ones. A missile-defense system cannot be tailored to protect some people and not others.

Second, the idea offends our sense of justice. Suppose that we could convert defense into a private good. The defense system would then defend only those who bought its services. Presumably the more you bought, the better you would be defended. Few believers in democracy would like to see our national defense converted into a bastion for the rich. Nor would we remove from public use the law courts, the schools, the police, and so on. Unlike private goods, which we have the privilege of buying from our incomes, public goods are thought of as our rights. We are not willing to tell people that they must die on the streets since they cannot pay for health care.

There are valid arguments and clever techniques for returning some public goods into the market's fold. Historically it was difficult to imagine charging a toll for each city street, but with bar codes on cars and sensors spread around town, what was before too expensive and cumbersome to contemplate might now be feasible! The main point to keep in mind is that it is impossible to make all goods private, and for the ones that should remain public, the market cannot be used to establish a desirable level of output. Here the market mechanism must give way to a political method of making economic decisions.

THE MARKET IN REVIEW

We should keep in mind one theme of this chapter. It is that a market system has weak spots or ineffective areas peculiar to its institutional nature. The remedy requires political intervention of one kind or another—regulation, taxation, or subsidy—for there is no recourse other than political action when the self-regulating economic mechanism fails.

This is not a conclusion that should be interpreted as a kind of general plea for more government. Many economists who severely criticize the market want less government—certainly less bureaucratic, nonparticipatory, nondemocratic government. The point, however, is to recognize that the existence and causes of market malfunction make *some* government intervention inescapable. We can then seek to use government power to repair individual market failures in order to strengthen the operation of the system as a whole.

After so much criticism of the market system, perhaps it is well to conclude by recalling its strengths. Basically they are two. *First, the market encourages individuals to exert energies, skills, ambitions, and risk-taking in the economic pursuits of life. This gives to the market system a high degree of flexibility, vitality, inventiveness, changefulness.* For all their failures, the market economies have displayed astonishing growth, and the source of that growth lies ultimately in the activities of their marketers. No other system has been made to work in today's world. All high-income countries use market economies as the basic mechanism for producing economic welfare.

Second, the system minimizes the need for government supervision, although for reasons we now understand it cannot dispense with it. It would be a mistake to suppose that every instance of government intervention is an abridgement of freedom, or that every area of market activity is an exemplar of liberty. The truth is that government and market are equally capable of promoting liberty or giving rise to oppression. Nonetheless, in a world in which concentration of government power has historically been one of the greatest scourges of mankind, there is clearly a lot to be said for the existence of a mechanism capable of handling the basic economic tasks of society with but a minimal dependence on political authority.

FOURTEEN

The Two Worlds of Business

We have been talking about microeconomics in theory. Now is the time to get down to business—both little and big. Let's start with monopoly—and nowadays, oligopoly. These are bad words to most people, just as competition is a good word, although not everyone can specify exactly what is good or bad about them.* Often we get the impression that the aims of the monopolist are evil and grasping, while those of the competitor are wholesome and pure. Therefore the difference between a world of pure competition and one of monopoly seems to be one of motive and intent—the well-meaning competitor versus the ill-intentioned monopolist.

The truth is that exactly the same motives drive both the monopolist and the competitive firm. Both seek to maximize profits. Indeed, the competitive firm, faced with the need to watch costs closely in order to survive, may be more penny-pinching and profit-oriented than the monopolist, who can afford to take a less hungry attitude because he is not

---

*Pure monopoly is a rarity. Most "monopolistic" corporations operate in a market structure of oligopoly (a *few* sellers) rather than monopoly (only *one* seller). In an oligopolistic market a few sellers divide up the bulk of the business, and a long tail of smaller firms share the leftovers. For example, in the soap industry, the four biggest producers supply about 60 percent of all demand, and some six hundred-plus producers share the rest. Similarly, over one hundred companies make auto tires and tubes, but the top four do two thirds of total business.

so close to the edge. In a word, bad motives have nothing to do with the problem of less-than-perfect competition.

Then what is so good about competition? In theory the answer is clear: In a purely competitive market, the consumer is king. Indeed the rationale for such a market is often described as *consumer sovereignty.*

The term means two things. First, in a pure competitive market the consumer determines the allocation of resources by virtue of his or her demand—the public calls the tune to which the businessman dances. Second, the consumer enjoys goods that are produced as abundantly and sold as cheaply as possible. In such a market, each firm is producing the goods the consumer wants, in the largest quantity and at the lowest cost possible.

In a monopolistic or oligopolistic market the consumer loses much of this sovereignty. Firms have *strategies,* including that of increasing consumer demand for their particular products by describing them as different from, and better than, those of their competitors. If its advertising is successful, a firm will be able to sell its product at a price higher than the purely competitive one—a price that contains an element of monopoly because, however small the additional profit, it represents a return over and above that of a truly competitive setting.

THE COSTS OF IMPERFECT COMPETITION

No one contests these general conclusions. Prices in an "imperfectly competitive" market, where advertising seeks to make each product seem unique, will be higher than in a market where all products are obviously the same. Because they cost more, the volume of goods sold in such an imperfectly competitive market will be less than that sold in a perfectly competitive one.

But how important are these imperfections in actuality? Here the problem becomes muddier. Take the question of consumer demand. In 1867 we spent an estimated $50 million to persuade consumers to buy "name brand" products of all kinds. By 1900, advertising expenditures were $500 million. Today they are roughly $130 billion, about a third as much as we spend on all primary and secondary education. Indeed, advertising expenditures can be considered a kind of campaign to educate individuals to be good consumers, buying a different set of goods than they would have if the advertising did not exist.

To what extent does this infringe on consumer sovereignty? The question is perplexing. Once we go beyond a subsistence economy it is no longer possible to think of consumers as having "natural" tastes. For that reason, at least some advertising serves a genuinely educational purpose. Back in the 1910s people had to be educated into thinking that an ordinary family like themselves could actually own a car. Not so long ago, our parents had to be educated to think that flying was not only fast, but comfortable and safe.

Moreover, not all advertising works. In the 1950s, the Ford Motor Company spent a quarter of a billion dollars to persuade people that a new car called the Edsel was exactly what everyone had been looking for. Despite the barrage of ads, people looked the other way. Every year brings advertising fiascos of one kind or another.

Yet it is obvious that not all advertising serves a useful purpose. It is impossible to watch the raptures of "housewives" extolling different brands of soap, laxatives, or canned goods without thinking that perhaps the single most persuasive message of these minidramas is that grown-ups will say things they obviously don't really believe because they are paid money to do so. Is that perhaps the residual effect of advertising on our culture, including, not least, on our children?

So we find ourselves in a quandary. Few consumers would like to have the absolutely standardized outputs that would do away with the need for advertising, and most consumers accept the make-believe of advertising as a mildly irritating, occasionally useful, interruption of their TV watching. From the advertisers' standpoint, advertising is one big expense, but one that must be undertaken if a firm selling brand-name goods is to survive in a "competitive" world, however "imperfect" economists may call that kind of market.

What is the answer to this dilemma? Here is where the economists' claim to expertise ceases. The question is properly referred to experts on culture or morality, or to the collective wisdom of consumers themselves when they put on their political caps and vote for more or less government regulation of markets. As economists we are bound to raise these questions, but we would be overstepping our bounds if we presume to answer them.

What about the second main attribute of consumer sovereignty—the ability to buy goods as cheaply as possible? To what extent does oligopoly introduce inefficiency into the system?

Once again the evidence in fact is murkier than in theory. For one thing, we tend to leap to the conclusion that a competitive firm is also an efficient one. Is this really so? Suppose that the competitive firm cannot afford the equipment that might lead to economies of large-scale production. Suppose it cannot afford large expenditures on research and development. Suppose its workers suffer from low morale and therefore do not produce as much as they might.

These are not wild suppositions. There is good evidence that many large firms are more efficient, in terms of productivity per man-hour, than small firms, although of course some large, monopolistic firms tolerate highly inefficient practices simply because of the lack of competition. Big businesses generate higher rates of technical progress than small, competitive firms, and may well justify their short-run monopoly profits by long-run technical progress.

Once again, however, we must consider the other side. Profits in oligopolistic industries as a whole are 50 to 100 percent higher than those in competitive industries. In certain fields, such as over-the-counter medicines, there is evidence that consumers are sometimes badly exploited. Brand-name aspirins sell for up to three times the cost on non-brand versions, but few buyers know that they are paying more for an *identical* product. Certain medicines, such as antibiotics and the like, have enjoyed enormous profits—which is to say, have forced consumers to pay far more than they would have had to pay were the rate of profit a competitive one—but here the issue becomes more complicated. Patents, and hence monopoly profits, are given to firms deliberately to encourage them to invent new drugs. We make a trade-off—more expensive drugs today for more drugs tomorrow.

To turn the coin over once more, a further complication is introduced by virtue of the fact that oligopolies often have provided more agreeable working conditions, more handsome offices, and safer plants than have small competitive firms. Thus some of the loss of consumers' well-being is regained in the form of workers' well-being. Needless to say, this is not solely the result of a kindlier attitude on the part of big producers, but reflects their sheltered position against the harsh pressures of competition. Nonetheless, the gains in work conditions and morale are real and must be counted in the balance.

BIG BUSINESS

This is a good point to turn from little to big business, and competition is a good place to start. As we have said, competition is the driving force behind capitalist efficiency. "Survival of the fittest" was a phrase invented to describe this process, later borrowed by Darwin to depict the process of evolution. Firms make larger profits by driving others out of business and thereby getting a bigger market share. By the logic of the process, those who succeed grow.

As a curious result, a successful capitalist economy systematically generates pressures that weaken the driving force that is the secret of its success! Successful enterprises often gain monopoly or oligopoly power that allows them to raise prices and further increase profits. In a world of big business, winners make money by extracting monopolistic rents from their customers.

Despite preaching the virtues of competition, no capitalist firm wants to live in a competitive world, and this is as true of big firms as small ones. The difference is that there isn't much a small firm can do about it, whereas big business can try—and can often succeed to some extent—to put itself "above" the competition: "There is no firm like us!" boasts the big corporation, true or not. No corner drugstore can say as much for itself.

Around the world, governments' answer to the problem of big business power has been an attempt to restore competition, or at least to lessen the exploitation of consumers, by imposing antitrust laws, various regulations, and public ownership of key industries. In the United States, for example, regulations were imposed by Congress to curb the monopoly power of the railroads in the last half of the nineteenth century and antitrust laws were passed to break up the trusts in oil, copper, and steel. Public ownership appeared much earlier in the postal service, and later in the ownership of airports, but was never used to the extent that we find in Europe where, for example, the railroads have been, virtually from the start, built and operated by government.

How successful have been these efforts to limit the power of big business? With some exceptions—European railroads have been spectacularly successful—results have been disappointing, especially with regard to antitrust and regulatory legislation.

The reasons are various. Early on, it became apparent that enforcement agencies, such as the Interstate Commerce Commission, could gradually be captured by representatives of the regulated industries themselves. Indeed, railroad managers found useful careers in shuttling back and forth between being regulators and regulated. In Europe something similar happened when it became clear that publicly owned monopolistic corporations, such as the French Renault auto company, acted remarkably like privately owned monopolistic firms, such as the Peugeot company. More recently in our increasingly globalized world (into which we will look a few chapters ahead) it is clear that applying antitrust laws would have the unwanted effect of encouraging success-ful companies, like Microsoft, to set up branches abroad, while leaving more space for foreign companies to set up branches here. Whatever the result for world GDP, the United States could well be a loser. Hence, using antitrust laws, or attempting to coordinate antitrust action among nations, often gains editorial enthusiasm but rarely political support. Governments themselves no longer believe in its efficacy.

Last but not least, it is also possible to argue that oligopolistic problems are self-correcting. Technical change is often a cause for the creation of big business power, as we will see, but it can also be a powerful enemy of it. Of the twelve largest industrial firms in America in 1900, only one—General Electric—is alive today. For much the same reason, a fa-mous and lengthy antitrust case against IBM was dropped by the gov-ernment when it became apparent that the newly developed personal computer had transformed a once monopolistic industry into a highly competitive one. If one looks at the splitting up of AT&T, it is again clear that technology has accomplished what the government set out to do.

Moreover, it is important to recognize that American firms are far from being the world's largest. Only three of the ten biggest companies in the world, and seven of the largest twenty, are American. Breaking up an American giant firm for the benefit of a foreign one is hardly at-tractive—it merely transfers monopolistic profits that used to go into American pockets into foreign ones. Here, too, we must recognize that in a global economy a firm can be very big at home but still have to contend with a fierce competitive environment. General Motors is America's biggest firm, but in the worldwide market for cars its market power is vanishingly small. Indeed, one sometimes has the feeling that in a global world the fate of the monopolist may be that of the dinosaur.

As a result of all these factors, governments are deregulating and privatizing, rather than the other way around. In the United States, the airline, trucking, and telecommunications industries are being deregulated, and in Great Britain, France, and elsewhere abroad, airlines, airports, telecommunications, and even some rail transport is being privatized. Antitrust laws remain, but the heart has gone out of their enforcement. Ironically, antitrust legislation is being used today by private companies who wish to sue each other when they think one of their competitors has too much market power. Put bluntly, antitrust laws are now used more for private blackmail than for public purposes.

As a result, at the moment there is little consensus about what, if anything, should be done about big firms.

SMALL IS BEAUTIFUL—SOMETIMES

In the last two decades the assertion has often been made that most of the jobs in America are being created by small businesses and that, as a result, such business should be seen as the engines of national economic success. By implication, nothing else is necessary or important. Such assertions are neither factually correct nor economically true.

What creates jobs are not small businesses as such, but small businesses that grow large (Wal-Mart, Hewlett Packard, Microsoft). What are often counted as thousands of individual small firms, such as Mc-Donaldses—the nation's largest single private employer—are in reality giant integrated enterprises. Not surprisingly, these large firms usually pay higher wages, provide more generous fringe benefits, and offer better jobs than small businesses. At any time, the bigger the firm, the more likely it is to be a comparatively desirable employer. Perhaps more important, large firms are the source of most of the nation's private research and development. If big firms were privatized, much of the steady advance in technology and research would disappear.

Two last pluses. First, big firms provide most of the markets for small firms. Selling directly to millions of consumers in an era of large retail chains requires advertising budgets beyond the reach of small businesses. Big business is often the link between small individual suppliers and a mass market beyond their reach. Second, small high-tech firms are often spin-offs from large high-tech firms. A clever employee discovers something that is too small for a large firm to manage efficiently or which does not fit into its overall plans. Such employees take their clever ideas, which they have developed while working in the big firm, and go start up their own small companies. As a result, if the large firms did not exist, many small ones would never come into existence. Thus, large and small companies coexist in a complex symbiosis. Big firms can be the deadly enemy of small ones; they can also be their shelters and their mothers and fathers. What is beautiful in an economy is not smallness as such, any more than bigness. It is a mix of firms of many sizes, each performing the task that suits its size best.

A NEW SOCIAL CONTRACT?

In recent years, social dissatisfaction with large firms has not focused on their monopolistic powers to raise prices and deprive consumers of real spending power, but on their ruthless downsizings and the wage and fringe-benefit reductions they have forced upon their employees. Profits go up, not by raising prices, but by forcing wages down.

Today management seems to be imposing a new arrangement on labor. In the post–World War II boom, many profitable firms shared their gains with their employees in the form of annual wage raises for production workers, often including generous fringe benefits, plus a more or less clear understanding with white-collar employees that they could count on lifetime employment in addition to their raises, providing their performance was satisfactory. Moreover, when blue-collar workers had to be let go during slumps, they knew they would be the first to be rehired when things improved. Union contracts set the basic wage scale, revised every three years or so, but the annual wage and salary raises, and the lifetime employment arrangements, were parts of an unwritten "social contract"—that is, a tacit mutual understanding that set the relationship between employers and employees.

In the last decades a very different social contract has emerged. Large, profitable firms have laid off workers in droves—over 500,000 in some years—most of them white-collar workers. Those same firms are cutting wages and fringe benefits for their workers who do remain. Wage premiums are no longer paid for loyalty or past performance. Wages for engineers are adjusted downward if foreign engineers can be hired more cheaply. Within the firm, wage differentials are expanding rapidly. As we will see in our next chapters, CEOs make much more relative to average workers than they did twenty years ago. Those laid off will not be recalled when demand picks up.

Thus management by "stick" replaces management by "carrot." In the short run, fear is an effective management technique. But there is a lot of evidence that it does not work in the long run. Voluntary cooperation is necessary to make any human institution work, and the willingness to cooperate does not flow from fear. In downsizing, workers are being told that management feels no loyalty to them, and as a result they feel no loyalty to their firms.

From a hard-core economic perspective this is not surprising. The theory of profit maximization has always called for cost (wage) minimization. Fundamentally, labor and management aren't on the same team. Forcing wages down to the lowest possible levels is one of the functions of the capitalist. This is clear in a world where workers are unskilled and where productivity gains come from more capital-intensive production processes. From the perspective of economic theory the puzzle is not why firms started reducing wages in the late 1990s, but why they didn't start reducing them and cutting back on other benefits immediately after the war was over. Some have suggested that the answer was political—a fear that workers might feel sympathy for a socialist economic system that enjoyed a much higher repute in the days before the collapse of the Soviet Union than it does today.

Whatever the reason, the changing world production would seem to call for different behavior. In this world a firm's competitive edge comes not from having more physical equipment than its competitors but from having a more skilled work force that can create and operate the new man-made brain power industries. Since skills cannot be owned in a world without slavery the capitalist cannot "own" his only source of long-run competitive advantage in this world. He somehow has to attach those skills and that knowledge to the firm—or so one would think. In creating complicated new products, teamwork becomes central—no single genius knows enough to do it alone. Accordingly, today's firms test for, and preach the virtues of, teamwork skills.

It is precisely here that capitalism faces a fundamental fault line. Just when firms should be deciding who their key knowledge workers are and how these workers can be attached to the firm's long-run strategic objectives, many are doing exactly the opposite. In the downsizing process they are telling these same key workers that they should forget team loyalty and think only of themselves.

Metaphorically the firm will fire those who plant apple trees, once the trees are in the ground. It won't allow the planters to harvest the crop they have planted. They in turn are being told implicitly that they should quit right in the middle of apple-planting time, no matter how much they are needed, if someone else offers them a job paying even a small amount more. Their sacrifices in the past won't be remembered in the future.

Where this internal contradiction is apt to show up first is within the ranks of management itself. In the 1960s young managers would have told you that the route to personal success was to find a great company and be a good team player. If you told that to the young managers of the 1990s, they would laugh at you. Downsizing has delivered a very different message and created a very different ethos. The current belief is that the only route to success is ruthless self-interest and short-run salary maximization. Top managers increasingly have younger managers under them who don't believe in the team ideals that they preach but don't practice.

Perhaps fear and cynicism can be made into a successful long-run management philosophy, but it is unlikely. That combination did not work under communism and it is unlikely to work under capitalism. This is a challenge of great importance for this country. We will return to it more than once in the chapters to come.

IV

PROBLEMS

FIFTEEN

The Specter of Inflation

With this chapter we encounter the first of the problems that set this edition so sharply apart from the one that preceded it. We call it the *specter* of inflation, because in our last edition inflation was anything but a specter. Indeed, its causes and consequences and possible cures were realities that permeated a good deal of our book.

Today, inflation appears in a different guise. It is still with us in the sense that the prices of most things tend to go up a little each year, but that rate of rise has declined dramatically since inflation became a national threat in the 1970s. In 1980 consumer prices were rising at the rate of 13 percent a year, enough to double the cost of living every five to six years! In 1982 that rate had been cut in half, still enough to double the cost of living in less than a decade. Ten years later the yearly rise had been cut to 3 percent—a big improvement, but not so much that people weren't nervous about it. In fact, for 1997 the Consumer Price Index (CPI) showed a yearly rise of only 2.2 percent, the lowest since 1965. If we make adequate allowances for improvements in the quality of many goods, for all intents and purposes the inflation problem seems to be licked.*

---

*As we write these pages, there is considerable discussion as to the confidence that can be placed in the consumer price index. The question is the accuracy with which the index reflects changes in the cost of living beside the ups and downs in the *prices* of what we buy—namely, changes in the quality of what we buy. Is the higher price of today's new car, compared with yesterday's, the only thing that affects our standard of living? What

But if inflation is effectively banished from the system, why do we introduce its specter as the first of those disturbing problems that are the central purpose for this edition?

THE ROOTS OF INFLATION

Let us begin from an elemental but often overlooked fact of economic life. It is that capitalist economies are always in a state of nervous tension, of actual or potential movement, of overt or latent disequilibrium. Wars, changes in political regimes, resource changes, new technologies, shifts in consumers' tastes—all constantly disturb the tenor of business life. Ask any businessman if he lives in a calm pond or a choppy lake.

It may not seem important to begin from a stress on this deep-seated vulnerability characteristic of capitalist systems. But once we place the fact stage center, a striking question immediately faces us: how does it happen that the vulnerability results in inflation, and not depression or some other malfunction? For when we think of it, it was not inflation but other kinds of dysfunction that troubled capitalism in previous periods—think of the slump of 1893: six years of unemployment ranging from 12 to 18 percent of the labor force; or the collapse of the 1930s, with unemployment rates up to nearly 25 percent! Or recall the traumatic emergence of the new giant industrial trusts in the late nineteenth century, pushing up like corporate icebergs and cracking the floe of small enterprises of that time.

From this perspective, inflation appears as the way in which the capitalist system responds to shocks and disruptions in the institutional setting of the late twentieth century. Take, for example, the impetus given to inflation from the famous "oil shock" of 1973, when the Organization of Petroleum Exporting Countries (OPEC) suddenly boosted the price from three to eleven dollars per barrel, followed by another

---

about the greater safety of today's car, which in effect gives us more for our money? And how about longer delays on our undermaintained highways, which in effect makes using a car more expensive? A trustworthy cost of living index is important because it is used to adjust Social Security payments, and the interest paid on the Treasury's new "inflation proof" bonds, or the fear of impending inflation. Conventional wisdom has it that our CPI is now rising at only about 2 percent a year, perhaps even less, but the fact is that we do not know if that measurement is correct. Our bet is that you will be reading and hearing about this for some time to come.

boost from thirteen to twenty-eight dollars per barrel in the wake of the Iranian revolution of 1980. But now suppose that comparable companies band together as a coal cartel and suddenly announce a fourfold increase in coal prices. Would such a coal cartel have produced inflation? The question is ludicrous. It would have brought on a massive depression. Coal mines would have closed, steel mills shut down, car loadings fallen. That imaginary but unchallengeable scenario then puts the right question: What happened between 1873 and 1973 so that the same shock—an abrupt rise in energy prices—produced depression in one era and inflation in another?

The question is not hard to answer. Far-reaching changes had taken place within the social and economic structure of capitalism all over the world. Of these, by far the most visible and important was the emergence of large and powerful public sectors. In all Western capitalisms, these public sectors pumped out 30 to 50 percent of all expenditures, sometimes even more. *These public expenditures provided a floor for economic activity that did not exist before.* In itself that was enough to shift a depression-prone world toward an inflation-prone one.

The floors of public expenditure do not prevent the arrival of all recessions, as we know from experience. The difference is that a market system with a core of public spending does not easily move from recession into ever-deeper depression. The downward tendency of production and employment is limited by the support of government spending such as Social Security, unemployment insurance, insurance of bank deposits, and the like. Cumulative, bottomless depressions change into limited, although recurring recessions.

A second aspect of the sea change that came over capitalism in the last century was the rise in private power. We saw it in the vast organizations—the icebergs—that dominated the waters of business and labor alike.

The emergence of massive institutions of private power made an important contribution to our inflationary propensity. A striking difference was that in the past inflationary peaks were regularly followed by long deflationary periods. Prices tended irregularly downward over most of the last half of the nineteenth century. Why? One reason is that the economy was much more heavily agricultural in those days, and farm prices have always been more volatile, particularly downward, than the prices of manufactured goods. Hence an industrial economy, just by virtue of being dominated by manufactures, is much less likely to have price declines than a farming economy. A second reason is that the character of the manufacturing sector also changed. In the early decades of the twentieth century, it was not unusual for big companies to announce across-the-board wage cuts when times were bad. In addition, prices declined as a result of technological advances, and as a consequence of the dog-eat-dog price wars that continually broke out among industrial competitors.

That is all part of a chapter of economic history largely written finis. Agriculture is now only a small part of GDP. Technology continues to lower costs, sometimes dramatically—look at what has happened to the computer during the last decade!—but until recently these lower industrial costs were offset by a "ratchet tendency" shown by wages and prices since World War II. A ratchet tendency means that prices and wages go up, but rarely or never come down—always excepting technological revolutions or market debacles. In normal times and normal business, we saw the ratchet at work. Concentrated business and union power, coupled with a general horror of cutthroat competition, meant that wages and prices generally moved in only one direction—up. Except that when business was bad and competition got nasty, big companies did not cut wages or salaries.

These changes help us understand why we have moved so far from the world of our parents and grandparents who worried about many economic possibilities, but not about inflation, to our own world, in which a susceptibility to inflation always seems to hover in the background.

But susceptibility is one thing and its advent another. To complete our brief history we need to know what started the process off, in the way that stock market panics or unforeseen business failures pulled the rug from under the system in the old depression days.

Probably the initial impetus was the boost to spending that followed from the Vietnam War, which was shortsightedly financed by borrowing rather than by taxing, no doubt because of the general unpopularity of our involvement. A second powerful stimulus to inflation in *other* countries arose when the United States used its then dominant power to force other nations to accept our dollars in lieu of gold in settlement of foreign obligations. This built up large holdings of dollar credits abroad that eventually fed back on our own price levels as foreign nations used their dollars to buy U.S. exports. We have already mentioned the dramatic effect of these oil shocks on the price level in the United States, and we have compared their inflation-creating effect with the depression-creating effects that would likely have accompanied an imaginary "coal shock" in the 1870s.

Now we must pay heed to a very important change that made oil shock so contagious. This was the effort of the government to protect Social Security pensioners by "indexing" their payments to the cost of living, once a year raising their pensions by an amount equal to the rise in the previous year's cost of living. Similar arrangements were soon extended to many wage and salary earners in big private institutions, so that as prices rose, so did employees' incomes. Alas, by supplying more purchasing power when the national interest required just the opposite, this well-meant effort to counter the effects of inflation only served to strengthen its persistence. A tax increase on inflation-swollen incomes would have served the national purpose more effectively, but tax increases are not vote-winning political policies.

Against all these built-in tendencies, how did we finally get out of the inflationary spiral? One of these was sheer good luck. The major inflation-generating forces during the 1970s were "outside" the system—exogenous shocks, in economists' language. Inflation gained a good deal of its underlying momentum from rising oil prices whose cause lay in the Middle East, not in our own economy. Also important was a consistent upward pressure of food prices, partly the consequence of serious food shortages in the underdeveloped world, partly the result of adverse weather. A third cause was the generally rising trend of many other raw material prices, pulled up by the worldwide boom. All these exogenous shocks acted as a constant inflationary stimulus whose effects were spread throughout the system by indexing arrangements.

Now comes the good luck. By the 1980s, all these pressures had disappeared. The OPEC cartel had set the price of oil so high that oil production soared, while oil consumption was dramatically economized. As a result, the price of oil fell from forty dollars a barrel to just above ten dollars. In the underdeveloped world, population growth gradually slowed down and agricultural production finally speeded up. With good weather as a big assist, long-persisting food shortages slowly gave way to exportable food "surpluses," with the consequence of falling agricultural prices. As the boom in the developed world lost its momentum in

the early 1980s, demand for raw materials slumped, sometimes disas-
trously; after correction for inflation, copper prices fell to levels below
those of the Great Depression.

Taken together, these exogenous developments cut the inflationary
pressure by at least half during the 1980s. But because none of these
developments was within the control of U.S. (or European) policymakers, we can only call this first reason for the decline of the inflationary
spiral good luck.

A second reason was tough policy. Everyone had always known that
there existed one sure cure for inflation. It was to send the economy deliberately into a really deep recession. Until the 1980s, however, no one
was prepared to try the medicine, because no one was prepared to risk
the political consequences of attempting such a cure.

The situation changed in the early 1980s, first under the administration of President Jimmy Carter, then with redoubled intensity under
that of President Ronald Reagan. Tight monetary policies pushed interest rates over 20 percent, with the *desired* consequence of a steep and
prolonged business recession. At 20 percent interest rates, small businesses found themselves unable to afford the normal loans needed to
provide them with working capital. Consumers were driven out of the
mortgage and household-appliance markets. Even the biggest corporations were themselves caught in a devastating squeeze as interest costs
mounted and as buyer demand declined.

Thus, as expected *and desired,* tight money brought on a recession.
By 1982, unemployment had passed the 11 percent mark; in Europe
unemployment soared even higher. As unemployment rose, wage
cuts—unheard of during the previous long boom—were instituted in
hard-pressed industries. And as the pressure of wage costs declined,
and the easy days of ever-expanding markets gave way to hard days of
stable or contracting markets, corporations were forced into strategies
that many economists thought had been permanently relegated to the
history books: They began to shave prices.

A final coup de grace was administered by the pressures of foreign
competition. As U.S. interest rates soared, foreigners began to move
their funds into high-yielding U.S. bonds. The inflow of capital thereupon drove up the price of dollars as foreigners exchanged their domestic currencies for the dollars needed to buy U.S. Treasury or other
securities. As the dollar rose in value, Americans went on a shopping
tour for foreign merchandise that could be bought in America at bargain-

basement prices. At the same time, foreigners found themselves unable to afford American goods, now priced out of sight. Thus the pressures of foreign competition provided another source of inflation-taming competition.

Psychologically inflation came to an end with the crash in asset values in the late 1980s and early 1990s. Stock markets crashed in Japan and Taiwan. The fall in the Japanese stock market in real terms was even bigger than that in the American stock market from 1929 to 1932. Housing and real estate prices fell dramatically in most of the world. A post–World War II era of ever-rising real estate prices was over.

Together, good luck and tough policy broke the back of inflationary expectations. Double-digit inflation disappeared. Single-digit inflation subsided until a noninflationary world was once again in sight. This brings us back to the opening page of this chapter, in which we watched the gradual fading away of what was once a very real and very dangerous inflationary threat.

THE SPECTER EMERGES

So the Great Inflation came to an end—rather ignominiously, but an end just the same. And what about the Great Inflationary Propensity? That, too, takes a brief historical word. We got out of the Great Depression by the spending generated by the advent of World War II. But not until the 1950s did we lay in the structure to prevent *another* Great Depression, mainly by the extension of Social Security, unemployment insurance, and a welfare support system. The efficacy of those measures is shown by the fact that two back-to-back recessions in 1980 and in 1981 did not bring on the cumulative collapse characteristic of the economy's behavior in the presupport days.

We would seem, then, to be in the best of all worlds today—the Great Inflation lies behind us, an effective antidepression program in place, and we have seen the evaporation of the forces that made us so inflation prone in the 1980s. Now, however, comes the first of those disturbing changes that are a major reason for this new edition. The change lies in one further effect of the Great Inflation that we have left unmentioned until now. It is that an anti-inflationary viewpoint has become something like an obsession on the part of most economic policymakers. Above all, this frame of mind has found its spokesmen in the central bankers of the world, who hasten to put on the monetary brakes at the first sign that the rate of unemployment may be exceeding what is assumed to be its proper rate, with the threat of rekindling inflationary tendencies. Hence, perhaps the most important legacy of the inflationary years following Vietnam and the oil shock is a tendency to look with suspicion on "too high" employment, with its consequence of "too rapid" economic growth! *Thus, the new problem we face is not inflation, but the specter of inflation.* We are paying for our successful fight against a very real inflationary condition in the past by denying ourselves the noninflationary growth that is both possible and much needed in a radically changed economic setting.

What allows economists like ourselves to dissent from the conventional central bank view? The first argument is that unemployment is, in fact, much higher than the official statistics show. These statistics only count as "unemployed" individuals who are actively looking for full time work, in vain. There are something like 7.5 to 8 million such workers—something between 5 and 5.5 percent of the total number of individuals in the work force itself. But that count does not include another 5 to 6 million jobless workers who have given up the search as hopeless: they are simply not considered "unemployed." Then there are another four-plus million who *are* working, but at part-time jobs because they cannot find the full-time employment they seek.

Add together these groups and the number of unemployed workers rises from the official count of around 5.5 percent of the work force to about 10 percent. Then there are still *another* 18 million workers who are in what might be called underemployment—working on call, or in temporary jobs, or as self-employed "contractors." Finally, there exist, somewhere or other, *another* nearly 6 million "missing" males—men of working age who exist in the national census but not in the statistics of the labor force. Presumably a good number of them would appear from their statistical limbo if good, steady jobs were around.

In all, then, the potential work force is much larger—perhaps as much as 15 percent larger—than the number that the Fed takes to be our bulwark against an inflationary explosion of "over-full" employment. The fact that we have found jobs for some 20 million workers since 1985—about the number we need to absorb legal immigration and natural growth of the working force as children come of working age—seems impressive until we take into account these overlooked or unmentioned numbers.

Thus the first of our new problems is that the country is being denied much needed potential growth because of a specter—the threat of an inflation that is very unlikely to occur.

Does that mean that the scourge of inflation has finally been laid to rest, like the once dreaded prospect of a "bottomless" depression? No one could be so brash in the face of the possibilities for a new rearmament boom, another oil shock, or some such dangerous inflation-breeding misfortune. But these are possibilities, not likely prospects—and we know from experience how to limit their self-feeding dangers.

Meanwhile, in addition to the presence of a very large unrecognized body of the "un- or under-" employed, there are other reasons to doubt that inflation constitutes a clear and present danger. International competition has increased at all levels, as we shall see when we study globalization. American firms have much less price-setting power. New kinds of technology permit dramatic cost-cutting, including labor costs. Together these forces have produced a world in which real wages are eroding steadily. It is difficult to construct a plausible inflationary scenario in such conditions.

At the same time, the specter of inflation is regularly invoked to limit increases in government spending for such purposes as pensions and health care benefits for the elderly. This reluctance to allow government spending to rise because of its presumed inflationary consequence has meant a cutback in projects on education, infrastructure, research and development—the very areas of public spending most likely to generate prosperity in the future. So, too, within the private sector slow growth leads business firms to cut back on plant and equipment investments as well as skills training for their work forces. Underemployed workers similarly don't see the payoffs they need to justify investments in their own education. As a result the war on inflation leads to squeezing out precisely the public and private investments that are necessary to create future prosperity.

So all things considered, it seems to us that the Age of Inflation has come to an end, and that our present need is to prevent its memory from standing in the way of strengthening the programs aimed at dealing effectively with the challenges of tomorrow. That is why we say that it is not inflation, but the specter of inflation, that constitutes the first of our new problems. We shall have to wait to see how effectively we will deal with it.

SIXTEEN

The Inequality Problem

If you ask most people why one person's income is larger than another's, they will probably answer—assuming that the person in question isn't the recipient of a large inheritance or the victim of circumstances such as discrimination—that people "earn" the incomes they get. What they mean is that individuals generally are believed to get back from society some rough equivalent of what they give to it.

Economists make the same claim, in more sophisticated language. They assert that incomes by and large reflect the "marginal productivities" of different contributors to the economic process, which is only a more complicated way of saying that individuals tend to receive incomes that approximate the value of the work they perform for others or for themselves, where "value" depends upon a complicated mixture of an individual's supply of talents, skills, drive, risk taking, and hours of leisure forgone relative to the market's demand for those same elements.

Does this explanation help us understand the actual distribution of incomes we find in society? The answer, as many times before, is yes and no. It throws some light on matters because in many cases a person's productivity obviously bears on his or her income: Skilled workers make more money than unskilled ones. But there also is to be a lot more variance in earnings than measured differences in productive contributions would predict. Good and bad luck—such as being with the right company that is expanding or the wrong company that is downsizing—makes a lot of difference.

THE TOP AND THE BOTTOM

Let's start with the top and bottom of the income scale—in reverse order. Back in Chapter Three, we took a quick look at the dimensions and characteristics of poverty. One thing that stands out immediately is the heavy incidence of poverty among black families and families headed by women. How do economists explain that? They don't. They turn to historians and sociologists to explain the current effects of a history of slavery and discrimination and the sharply rising incidence of female-headed families.

Once poor, a vicious poverty trap takes over. People are poor because they do not have the skills to be productive, but being poor, they don't have the funds to acquire the skills necessary to be productive. Without working-adult role models, poor work habits develop among the young that make it impossible to get work—leading to another generation without working-adult role models. Cause and effect get hopelessly entangled.

Many of those who are poor have also either been pushed out of, or dropped out of, the work force and have become dependent upon government transfer payments for much of their income. Public generosity, or lack of generosity, has more to do with their incomes than individual productivities.

What about the other end of the income scale, the top-most echelon of millionaires? Can marginal productivity help us explain high incomes? At this level earnings cease to be important and wealth or capital income dominates.

Since about half of the superrich have inherited their wealth, individual merit clearly cannot explain much of what is observed. But what about millionaires who have earned their fortunes? Can we explain their wealth by their productive contribution to society? Yes, but not in the conventional way that looks at the marginal productivity of work effort or capital.

In micro-economic theory, individuals get wealthy by saving, not consuming, and by earning market rates of interest upon those savings. Those market rates of interest in turn reflect the marginal productivity of capital. Undoubtedly some persons do accumulate modest sums by refraining from consumption, but they do not accumulate fortunes. If you start with $100,000, earn a real (inflation corrected) rate of return of 2 percent (1996's rate), and pay income taxes on your interest, it takes a long time (about twenty-six years) to pile up even $1 million. In contrast, most of the superrich accumulate their fortunes very rapidly. Bill Gates became the United States's richest man with $29 billion in less than two decades. How does someone become rich overnight?

Suppose that an entrepreneur figures it will cost $1 million to build and equip a plant to make a newly patented product. The product should sell at a price that will bring a profit of $300,000. A bank puts up the money. The plant is built and the expected $300,000 profit is realized. Now comes the instant fortune. To the nation's capital markets, the actual cost of the plant is of no consequence. What counts is the rate of return on investments *of the same degree of risk*. If that rate is 10 percent, the investor's plant is suddenly worth $3 million, for this is the sum that will yield $300,000 at a 10 percent return. The inventor is now worth $2 million, over and above what he owes to the bank. He will have risen to the status of an instant millionaire because the financial markets will have capitalized his profits into capital gains.

If the market is big enough to absorb more of his products than can be produced in his one existing factory, he will be worth even more when he sells shares in his company to the public, since those shares will reflect the value of both his current investments and his future investment opportunities. His wealth does not reflect the marginal productivity of his work effort or the marginal productivity of his capital, but the value of the niche that he has been able, or lucky enough, to create for his products.

Leaving the very rich and the very poor aside, most Americans depend upon earnings from work to provide them with essentially all of their income. Much of what we see reflects individual productivities. As even a quick glance at the following table shows, there is a strong relationship between education and earnings.

MALE EDUCATION AND AVERAGE EARNINGS, 1996

High school	
1–3 years	$17,664
4 years	$25,056
College	
1–3 years	$29,136
4 years	$42,240
Graduate School	$50,304

Source: U.S. Bureau of the Census

The explanatory power of productivity is obvious if we look at the incomes of top-earning lawyers and pilots and artists and TV newscasters, and the contribution they make to output. We may think it "not right" that sports and rock stars make so much (and others, like nurses, so little) but that's not to deny that by market criteria their contribution to society is large. No one has to buy their videos or watch their performances. We voluntarily pay a lot of money to do so.

At the same time the linkage between productive skills and earnings is not nearly as tight as is often implied. Around each of those median earnings for different levels of education in the previous table there is a wide distribution of actual results. For example, between forty-five and fifty-four years of age (the peak earning years), 26 percent of white high-school graduates will end up making more money than the average white male college graduate, and 21 percent of college graduates will make less than the average high-school graduate. What pays off on average does not necessarily pay off for every individual.

The complexities of the system for distributing earnings can be seen by looking at the factors that underlie recent dramatic shifts in the distribution of earnings. Between 1973 and 1995, real per capita GDP rose by 39 percent—not a remarkable rate of increase, but not an unsatisfactory one either. The trouble was that it wasn't shared evenly. The top 20 percent of the work force did very well, because it captured nearly all of the nation's gains in earnings. But the earnings of nonsupervisory workers—the 80 percent of the work force that doesn't boss others—went down by 14 percent, male pay falling more than female. The historical truth neatly conveyed in President John F. Kennedy's phrase "A Rising Tide Lifts All Boats" ceased to be true.

THE FORCES AT WORK

Clearly, these changes were not all caused by sudden adverse changes in individual productivities. Powerful forces were at work also. One of them, to which we will turn again in our next chapter, was the development of the technologies of transportation and telecommunications that lay behind the phenomenon of globalization. As more and more American firms moved parts of their operations abroad, many high-waged employments disappeared here, to reappear at much lower wages halfway around the globe. What economists call "factor price equalization"—a tendency for the wages of equi-skilled jobs to rise in low-wage countries and to fall in high-wage ones—weighed heavily against the earnings of former steelworkers, and skilled or semiskilled assembly-line workers in other industries. There was still a vast gulf between the levels of earnings in the U.S. and in India, but the forces at work were no longer lifting all boats, but raising some and lowering others.

At the same time, the new technologies were also working against the lower-paid portion of the work force. Computers and automated production methods made it possible to dispense with the old-fashioned factory supervisor and to put responsibility for a smooth flow of work more directly into the hands of work teams. But the team members had to be better educated to handle the new decision-making responsibilities. Just-in-time inventory control made obsolete the traditional (and expensive) need for "backups" of spare parts, but it also required workers with higher levels of mathematical sophistication—as did new statistical quality-control techniques. As the demand for skilled workers rose and the need for unskilled workers fell, the wages for the two groups not surprisingly spread apart. Worst hit were white male high school graduates.

Seemingly distanced from these large-scale forces was a matter we have not directly considered. It was the plummeting in the power of the industrial unions. At their peak in 1954, unions represented almost 40 percent of workers in the private sector. By 1973, when wages were already weakening, union membership had dropped to under 30 percent. Today it is just over 10 percent. In the automobile industry, the steel industry, the construction trades—all longtime bastions of union strength—unions no longer play a key role in wage negotiations. They take what they can get.

Why did union strength plummet? One very important reason starting in the 1970s was a sharp decline in the place of manufacturing industries and in the strongly unionized companies that had dominated them. To take an instance, United States Steel found itself so seriously battered by new, more efficient, and much-smaller-scale ways of making steel that it was forced to diversify its operations, actually changing its name to USX to indicate that steel was no longer its central interest. Along with the change came an equally marked decline in the steelworkers' union which, unlike USX, did not find new fields to make up for the thousands of steelworker members it lost.

Finally, we must mention a development that was not perhaps the most serious "numerical" cause of declining union influence, but was crushing in its political and psychological effects. This was the reaction by President Reagan in 1981 to a strike called by the air traffic controllers' union, which embraced much of the personnel who directed air traffic across the United States. President Reagan simply fired the entire group, and the flight controllers found themselves replaced by nonunion operators. The shock was the recognition that the United States government could no longer be counted on as a strong supporter of unionization, a role it had played since New Deal days.

Thus there is no doubt that a decline in union power has been a major factor in explaining the fall in relative incomes of the working class, especially in industry. Today the union movement is trying to rebuild its strength, but it seems highly unlikely that labor will regain its former bargaining power in the foreseeable future. As a result it is difficult to imagine wages again reaching their former place in the spectrum of incomes. The forces bringing about inequality are not likely to disappear for the working person.

MEANWHILE, UP AT HEADQUARTERS . . .

But none of this yet touches what has certainly been the most dramatic aspect of the growing inequality of economic rewards over the last decades. This has been the skyrocketing of topmost incomes in the corporate sector. All through the 1970s the ratio of CEO remuneration to that of the average worker was just over 40 to 1. If we take an arbitrary figure of $25,000 as the average wage in that year, this meant that average CEO compensation was $1 million. By 1990 the ratio was 225 to 1. If we suppose for illustration's sake that average wages were then $35,000, average CEO pay approached $8 million.

What lay behind this unprecedented leap in executive compensation? Here, once again, we leave the relatively clear explanations of economics for the deeper but less certain insights of sociology and politics. We noted in our last chapter that during the 1950s and 1960s there may have been a belief held by management that workers might be seduced by the then rosy image projected by socialism abroad—a belief that may have led to what economists call "efficiency wages"—wages higher than those based on market forces, whose purpose was to maintain the loyalty and efficiency of corporate work forces. As part of this defensive strategy it is possible—we really have no hard evidence—that executives may have held back from paying themselves their full market value to retain the good will of their employees.

If the explanation is true, when the allurements of socialism disappeared with the fall of the Soviet Union, these defensive views disappeared with them. Efficiency wages went by the board, along with any worries or inhibitions that executives might have felt about paying themselves the best they could get. Perhaps related to this was the rise of what economist Robert Frank has called "winner take all" markets—markets in which modern technology, mainly TV exposure, allowed a few individuals to get extraordinary pay for their services, whether as pop singers, opera singers, or whatever. It would hardly be surprising if CEOs did not ask themselves whether they were not worth as much as Michael Jordan or Placido Domingo.

Yet another factor working to widen income disparities has been the search for, and the acceptance of, ever-wider income differentials as socially acceptable or even right. In the days of our Founding Fathers a hundredfold difference between one person's income and another's would have been regarded as a gross violation of ethical norms. By the mid-nineteenth century, the enlarged scope and growing personality of economic life steadily increased the acceptance of, even the admiration for, high rewards for economic success, as long as that success was attained by legal means. During the roaring twenties the sky was the limit, no questions asked. Something like this state of mind seems to have reappeared in our time: when the CEO of AT&T improved the profitability of his company by letting forty thousand employees go, his grateful stockholders rewarded him with a bonus of $15 million.

Thus there is no single reason that explains the growing distance between rich and poor. That the distribution has shown a remarkable change is beyond question: in 1976 the top 1 percent of families in the nation owned 22 percent of all family wealth. In 1992 the top 1 percent owned 42 percent. In this last figure, as well, we are back to the 1920s.

NATIONAL CHARACTER

Can we change this state of affairs? One thing is clear: because it is the consequence of many contributory causes, the remedy will require changes in tax structures, financial and other business practices, and not least, social standards.

That raises two last questions: first, do we want to encourage a more egalitarian distribution of income? Some economists approve of the existing one because they believe it will encourage saving among the top families and thereby encourage an investment boom that will, in the end, make us all better off. Not to conceal our own preferences, we doubt that an inegalitarian economy will promote overall well-being, because we place more faith in the propulsive effects of mass purchasing power than in the investment willingness—or extent—of a high-income minority.

But there is a second and more disturbing question: even if we would welcome a more level economic landscape, do we know how to bring it about? We have already called attention to the wide range of possible social and political, as well as economic, reasons for growing inequality, but one very important explanation remains to be considered. It is the difference in national attitudes with regard to acceptable income distributions. Looking around the developed world we find that the spread from top to bottom is much larger in the United States than in all the other advanced capitalisms.

Take the question of the shares of rich and poor in the most affluent nations in 1991. In Finland, the most egalitarian of these nations, the total income of the top 10 percent was 2.7 times greater than the total income of the bottom 10 percent. In Norway it was slightly more—2.8 to 1. In the Netherlands it was 2.9 to 1; in Canada, 3.8 to 1. In the United States it was 5.7 to 1. We had the dubious distinction of being the nation with the largest difference between rich and poor, comparing top and bottom deciles, not topmost and bottommost 1 percents.*

How can one explain this state of affairs? Are European executives less "rational" or "maximizing" than Americans? Or do they live in societies whose topmost executives or richest families feel themselves part of a larger social group—a national family—not a mere collection of individuals, each out for him- or herself?

The truth is that we cannot clearly explain why different nations have different views as to the norms that apply to themselves. All we know is that French capitalism is different from Italian, and Italian from Swedish, and Swedish from Japanese, and that these differences, deeply rooted in their histories, play powerful roles in determining what is acceptable in the structure of rewards—and what is not.

*Surenda Kushlik, *Challenge* magazine, Sept./Oct. 1996, p. 54.

This does not mean that these national patterns are unchangeable. Sweden, the model for egalitarian capitalist income distribution since the 1930s was in the late nineteenth century a country of little social conscience. The United States, whose tolerance of inequality has been the subject of our chapter, was, during the Roosevelt years, much more interested in reaching standards of national fairness than it is today. Hence, as political moods change, economic patterns are likely to follow suit.

The trouble, of course, is that we do not know how to change political sentiments at will —perhaps fortunately. Put differently, this means that political beliefs limit our economic ability to steer the ship of state as we may wish. Does this mean that American inequality is likely to remain with us for a very long time? That we doubt, but it suggests it may take a stimulus as serious as was the Great Depression to bring about the change of heart as well as mind needed to establish a new American pattern of rich and poor.

SEVENTEEN

Globalization

Of all the changes that have made explaining economics more difficult today than it was only a few years ago, none is more dramatic and more puzzling than what we call the globalization of the economy. Globalization is a new term, but the problem is by no means new. From the early eighteenth century on, economists have worried about the question raised by the economic interpenetration of nations, which is what globalization is essentially about. That which sets the problem apart in our time are two developments. First, globalization has appeared on a hitherto undreamt of scale. Second, it crucially involves a nation which not very long ago rarely stopped to consider its worldwide economic involvements. That country is the United States, today "globalized" to a degree we would not have imagined possible only a decade or so ago.

At the core of the problem of globalization is what appears to be a simple question: if two (or more) countries trade with one another, or produce goods and services in each others' territories, can both sides in the matter come out ahead, or will one side take advantage of the other? This was a question that Americans could discuss in a calm tone of voice at a time when our total foreign trade—our exports plus our imports—amounted to a mere 5 percent of GDP. It is not so easy to discuss today when imports plus exports exceed 25 percent of GDP, when Toyota and Honda are names as familiar to Americans as GM and Ford, and when we are uneasily aware of the $1.3 trillion-a-day market for money. A trillion dollars is a sum roughly as large as the total size of what we ordinarily think of as the stock of "American" money, but the new market for money is exclusively used to buy the foreign exchange connected with this thing called globalization.

Is this good for the United States? Bad for it? Irreversible? Controllable? It may help us prepare for the pages ahead to know that the answer to these questions will be: All of the above. But we cannot explain that answer until we have found out what globalization is about. That is what we will do in this chapter and the next, when the money flow comes up.

THE GLOBAL ECONOMY

Why has globalization suddenly burst upon us? In large part the answer lies in the technology of communication—we can talk to subordinates or colleagues, inspect a factory, arrange a loan, buy and sell commodities or shares virtually anywhere in the world by phone and computer screen. In part it is also the technology of transportation: air travel shrinks the world just as did steam engines and automobiles in the eighteenth and nineteenth and early twentieth centuries—only more so. The jet plane makes Beijing closer to New York than San Francisco was in the 1920s.

The result is the appearance of a truly global market—go read the labels in your neighborhood store: the tomatoes come from Mexico, the shirts from China, the computer software from India or maybe Taiwan, the wines from Chile or Australia. So-called "American" cars are full of foreign-made components. And everything we say about our markets is as true—or even more so—for Paris, Stockholm, Johannesburg. Economically speaking, we live in something that is very close to One World. The trouble is that politically, it isn't.

What's wrong with living in a world where you can shop in Tokyo or Buenos Aires without leaving home? For consumers it is very good. But for producers there are two troubles. One is that goods made at home often have to compete with goods made in countries that do not impose U.S. standards on their own producers, such as not using sweatshop or child labor, observing a forty-hour workweek, etc. Is that "fair competition" for those Americans who are trying to produce these goods at home?

Second question: If foreign goods displace U.S. ones because they are cheaper, what happens to the U.S. workers who lose their jobs? As we have seen, part of the process of globalization is that wages are driven down in higher-wage countries and (gradually) increased in lower-wage ones. The same is true of returns on capital. In a word, globalization is a great evener. Evening out can be trouble enough within a country. Between countries it is obviously much more troublesome.

For example, when we signed NAFTA—the North American Free Trade Agreement—with Mexico (and Canada) a few years ago, we knew that one consequence would be greatly increased pressure on U.S. garment manufacturers from Mexican-made goods, because Mexican wages are far below our own. That might have been all right had the agreement contained a commitment to relocate or retrain displaced U.S. workers for other employments. No such commitment was made, so that NAFTA *did* increase Mexican imports, as it was meant to do, but it also increased U.S. unemployment, as it was not meant to do. Partly this was because of Mexican financial problems—in early 1995 what had been a large trade surplus became a trade deficit. But precisely such rabbit punches are themselves part of the mutual interpenetrations that make a globalized economy much riskier than an old-fashioned multinational one.

Hence we can see that globalization changes our world because it increases economic competitiveness and political defensiveness. Is there a solution to this problem? It is part of the yes and no that makes the global problem difficult. We will come back to it in due course.

THE MULTINATIONALS

One more aspect of globalization needs a look. It is the appearance of a new principal agency of globalization itself, the multinational—sometimes called transnational—corporation whose business empires literally straddle the globe. Take PepsiCo, for example. PepsiCo does not ship its famous product around the world from bottling plants in the United States. It produces Pepsi Cola in more than five hundred plants in over one hundred countries. When you buy a Pepsi in Mexico or the Philippines, Israel or Denmark, you are buying a U.S. product that was manufactured in that country.

PepsiCo is a far-flung, but not a particularly large, multinational, in the top twenty U.S. companies ranked by sales. Compare it with the Ford Motor Company, a multinational that consists of a network of sixty subsidiary corporations, forty of them foreign-based. Of the corporation's profits in recent years, one third have come from abroad. And if we studied the corporate structures of GM or IBM or the great oil companies, we would find that they too are multinationals with substantial portions of their total wealth invested in productive facilities outside the United States. If we broaden our view to include the top one hundred U.S. firms, we find that at least two thirds have such far-flung production facilities. Moreover, the value of output that is produced overseas by the largest corporations is twice as large as the value of the goods they still export from the United States.

Another way of establishing the spectacular rise of international production is to trace the increase in the value of U.S. foreign direct investment; that is, the value of foreign-located, U.S.-owned plant and equipment (not U.S.-owned foreign bonds and stocks). In 1950 the value of U.S. foreign direct-investment abroad was $11 billion. Thirty-five years later it was over $1.5 trillion. Today it is nearly double that. Moreover, this figure too needs an upward adjustment, because it includes only the value of U.S. dollars invested abroad and not the additional value of foreign capital that may be controlled by those dollars. For example, if a U.S. company has invested $10 million in a foreign enterprise whose total net worth is $20 million, the U.S. official figures for our foreign investment take note only of the $10 million of American equity and not of the $20 million wealth that our equity actually controls. In general, something between a quarter and a half of the real assets of our biggest corporations are abroad. Effectively, U.S. big business is today world big business.

The movement toward the internationalization of production is not just a U.S. phenomenon. If the U.S. multinationals are today the most imposing (of the world's biggest 500 corporations, 153 are American), they are closely challenged by non-U.S. multinationals (141 of the biggest 500 are Japanese). Philips, for example, is a huge Dutch multinational company with operations in 150 countries. Of its 270,000 employees, most work in nations other than the Netherlands. Royal Dutch/Shell is another vast multinational, whose home is somewhere between the Netherlands and the United Kingdom (it is jointly owned by nationals of both countries). Another is Nestle Chocolate, a Swiss firm, almost every franc of whose revenues originate outside Switzerland. Measured by the size of the Swedish capital invested there, São Paulo is Sweden's second biggest industrial city! Fiat's auto division has 25 percent of its sales in Europe outside of Italy and another 40 percent in the rest of the world. Its New Holland agricultural equipment division has only 7 percent of its sales in Italy. Fiat manages seventy-six manufacturing plants outside of Italy.

A few years ago the United Nations surveyed the size of the world of the multinationals. Gerard Piel reports on their findings: "The 350 largest [multinationals] had a combined turnover of $2,700 billion in 1985. That was 30 percent of the entire GNP of the world market economy and larger by several hundreds of billions of dollars than the combined GNP of all the preindustrial economies, China included."* We do not have more up-to-date figures, but we know they would be bigger.

MULTINATIONALS AS SUPERNATIONALS

Multinationals are not to be thought of only as foreign enterprises seeking to invade someone else's market. They also include enterprises that have located branches abroad to invade *their own* markets. For example, much of the influx of automotive and other manufactures from Mexico into the United States arises from U.S. subsidiaries that have gone south to take advantage of low-wage costs there. Thus, the real challenge of the MNCs (multinational corporations) is their ability to move technology around the world. How does a country hold on to a technological edge if its own companies are transferring that technology to foreign sites? The question this raises is a new one for political economy: "Who is 'us'?"

What drives a firm to produce overseas rather than just sell overseas? One possible answer is straightforward. A firm is successful at home. Its technology and organizational skills give it an edge on foreign competition. It begins to export its product. The foreign market grows. At some point, the firm begins to calculate whether it would be more profitable to organize an overseas production operation. By doing so, it might get to know the local market better, could serve its customers better, and would save transportation costs. It may be able to evade a tariff by producing goods behind a tariff wall. A very important consideration is that it may be able to take advantage of lower wage rates. And so, gradually, it ceases shipping goods abroad and instead exports capital, technology, and management—and becomes a multinational.

*Gerard Piel, *Only One World* (New York: W.H. Freeman & Co., 1992), p. 246.

More and more of the great corporations of the world have come to consider their "natural" markets to be the globe, not just their home countries. The struggle in automobiles, in computers, in telecommunications, in steel is for shares of a world market. That is why we find companies such as IBM or General Motors considering the entire globe as their oyster, not only with regard to the "sourcing" of raw materials, but to the location of plants, and finally the direction of sales effort. With modern, highly organized systems of production and distribution, the manufacture of commodities is more and more easily moved to whatever country produces them most cheaply, whereas their sale is forced on the countries that represent the richest markets. Thus we have a transistor radio whose parts have been made in Hong Kong or South Korea or Singapore, assembled in Mexico, and sold in the United States—by a Japanese manufacturer!

This can have disconcerting results. Suppose a country wants to slow down its economy through monetary policies such as higher interest rates designed to reduce plant and equipment spending. A restrictive monetary policy at home may be nullified by the ability of a multinational to borrow abroad in order to finance its investment at home. Conversely, a monetary policy designed to stimulate the home economy may end up in loans that increase production in someone else's economy. Moreover, it is not easy to suggest that monetary policies should be coordinated among countries, since the economic needs of different countries may not be the same: what is right for one country at a given time may be wrong for another. Thus, stimulatory fiscal policies may increase the demand for goods and services but that demand may focus on imported products rather than products produced locally. In a word, the effectiveness of national economic policy-making weakens.

Thus the desire of nation-states to retain control over productive activity within their own borders runs up against the powerful counterthrust of transnational corporations looking for markets without much regard for national boundaries. Oddly, this new vulnerability works two ways. On the one hand, the multinational is in a position to win hard bargains from the host country in which it seeks to enter if the corporation is a bearer of new technologies and management techniques that the host nation seeks. On the other hand, once a multinational *has* entered a foreign nation, it becomes a *hostage* of the host country. It is now bound by the laws of that country and may find itself obliged to undertake policies different from those of its "home" country. At the same time, however, the nation of which it is now a hostage itself becomes hostage to the forces of world competition, often with disconcerting results. Take the case of Japan, where until recently it has been an unwritten law that workers engaged by large corporations would, after a trial period, become permanent employees. This practice was not easy for non-Japanese companies to match, insofar as the government only helped Japanese employers meet these additional costs.

But now comes a new twist as Japan finds itself increasingly pitted against the competition of new, up-and-coming countries that do not practice such generous wage contracts. As a result, following a deep recession in the late 1990s, Japanese firms found themselves abandoning their generous wage policies and turning to a much cheaper source of labor—part-time workers to whom no long-term obligations applied.

Or take the problem of a multinational that is forced by a fall in demand to cut back the volume of its output. A decision made along strictly economic lines would lead it to close its least profitable plant. But this may bring very serious economic repercussions in the particular nation in which that plant is located—so serious that the government will threaten to take action if the plant is closed. What dictates shall the multinational then follow—those of standard business accounting or those of political accounting?

The new problems that emerge were illustrated dramatically in the winter of 1994–1995 when both international financiers and Mexican citizens started moving massive amounts of money out of Mexico. To stem this outflow Mexico required large loans from the International Monetary Fund and the United States. To get the necessary loans Mexico had to accept the harsh monetary and fiscal policies that were dictated by the IMF and the U.S. Effectively, at least for a while, it lost control of its national economic policies and its sovereignty. In the summer of 1992, much larger and much wealthier countries (France, Italy, and Great Britain) faced similar problems. They too were forced to impose harsh monetary and fiscal policies to restore international "confidence."

The sovereignty issue arises in an acute form in regional trading groups such as the European Community or the North American Free Trade Association. If such groups are to be successful they must harmonize rules and regulations, as has already occurred in the European community with its fifty years of history. Firms need to compete on a level playing field where the regulations they face are the same from country to country. If harmonization did not occur, firms would simply move to the countries with the fewest rules and regulations. Yet each harmonization limits the power of national governments to change those same rules and regulations. Looming ahead in Europe lies the euro, the common currency to be established in 1999. If and when the euro comes into existence, national central banks, national abilities to set interest rates—even weak national currencies such as the Italian lira—may cease to exist.

THE FUTURE

Perhaps there was a point in the past where the development of a global economy might have been stopped by governmental actions. It did not happen in the aftermath of World War II partly because economic integration was seen as a way to lessen the probability of future world wars and partly because a global capitalistic economy was seen as necessary to contain communism. But for better or worse, the point of no return has been passed.

Today rapid improvements in transportation and communications are effectively pushing us closer together and creating a world economy regardless of what governments might attempt to do. Governments once controlled the movement of capital across national borders. But how does one control capital flows when money can be moved on a personal computer and when you and us can do a financial deal in the Bahamas without any of us being physically present in the Bahamas?

Powerful institutions such as multinationals and international financial markets now have enormous vested interests in the existence of a global economy. Those working in export industries would lose their jobs if global trade were to shrink. They and many others would fight any return to isolated national economies.

Today an American does not work in a U.S. economy. He or she works in a global economy where, even if one never leaves the United States, we buy from, sell to, or compete with, others who live elsewhere. Do we then live in a world in which powerful forces and institutions are in charge, and we citizens can only stand by passively as economic forces have their way? The answer, as we know, is Yes and

No. We have seen that globalization does indeed present new kinds of problems for which there exist no quick or easy remedies. But that does not mean that nothing can be done.

Downward wage pressures can be offset by micro-economic programs aimed at reskilling and reeducating workers with falling wages. Government investments in R&D and in public capital such as infrastructure can create more prosperous economies. In addition, to some extent at least, those who are injured by globalization can and should be compensated by those who are winners. The European Community, for example, is trying to create more trade among its members, while at the same time seeking to harmonize labor standards upward rather than downward. And of course it is proper for advanced nations to prohibit the importation of goods made by child or severely abused labor. There are human standards that are valid for poor and rich countries alike.

All these measures call for political skill, and ours is a book of economic explanations, not political wisdom. As we see it, our task is to point out that there is a positive as well as a negative side to the immense, apparently unstoppable force of global interpenetration. Just as macro and micro processes can be curbed and encouraged to yield socially better results than if they were allowed to run their course without legal and social constraints, we see globalization as a process that can be improved by deliberate intervention. The difficulties of finding acceptable and workable means of intervention in a multinational world need hardly be pointed out, but little is gained by making that the stopping point for discussion. We have no alternative but to live with the economic process of globalization as best we can, steering, softening, and channeling it with all the economic and political sense and sensibility we can muster.

The nature of the new problem raised by multinationals and global trade is not, at bottom, a question of a competitive struggle among national economies. The underlying issue is different. It is a struggle for a redefinition of national sovereignty itself. The real challenge posed by the multinationals and global trade is that the world's economic map does not neatly coincide with its political map. This raises the question of how national sovereignty will be protected or forfeited as the reach of international finance and production widens and deepens. The issue is not merely how the world's markets will be divided up, but the ways in which national sovereignty itself will be expressed in the twenty-first century.

EIGHTEEN

National Policy in a Globalized World

At the beginning of our previous chapter we noted, but did not look into, a remarkable phenomenon associated with globalization—the rise of a vast new market in currencies that dwarfs in size the mere $1 trillion that roughly constitutes what we ordinarily call the stock of our own money. To understand this new phenomenon, however, we must first become familiar with foreign exchange, because the new money of globalization consists not of any given currency, like dollars or francs, but the value of all the currencies together. Put differently, the size of the foreign exchange market represents the value, at any time, of all the moneys of different countries that have been exchanged for the moneys of other countries. In round numbers, over the course of any recent year, that sum comes to over $300 trillion. That does not mean that Americans have written checks for that amount in order to buy money of other countries. It represents, rather, the dollar equivalent of all the various currencies that have been bought and sold in currency markets around the world.

PRICING THE DOLLAR

For three decades after World War II most Americans never gave a thought to foreign exchange—that is, to what dollars were worth in other currencies and how that "price" of dollars was established. This was because the price of a dollar was one-thirty-fifth of an ounce of gold—a ratio declared by Congress—and the values of other currencies were fixed by their governments relative to that price. Occasionally foreign governments were forced to adjust the values of their currencies up or down relative to the dollar, but the dollar itself remained the Archimedian point on which the values of all other currencies depended.

All of this ended in 1970 when the dollar became a currency whose value would be determined by the supply and demand for it, like all other currencies. Millions of Americans who thought their dollar was as good as gold discovered that it was not. Sharp changes, up or down, in the value of the dollar became front-page news. What happened?

Let us begin by going back to the years just before 1985, when headlines told us that the dollar was soaring. Sometimes the headlines said that the yen or mark or pound had hit new lows. All these phrases meant the same thing—but what was that thing?

When the dollar is high on the international money markets, it does not mean that a dollar will buy more *U.S.* goods. That is a very important point to bear in mind. Our dollars are "high" in domestic purchasing power only to the extent that *domestic* prices fall, and they are low (or falling) in domestic purchasing power only insofar as our own prices rise.

When we speak of a "high" dollar in international trade, we mean something else—that a dollar will buy more francs, yen, or zlotys than before it rose. As a result, it becomes cheaper to buy more *foreign* goods or services. By way of turnabout, if the dollar is "low" in the international world, it buys fewer units of foreign currencies, so that foreign goods therefore cost us more.

Examples always help. How much would a twenty-franc French wine cost in America? The answer depends on the rate at which we can exchange dollars for the francs we need to pay the French producer. We discover the price by going to a dealer in foreign currency—usually a bank. If this were the mid-1980s, we would discover that we could get almost ten francs for each dollar. A twenty-franc bottle (ignoring transportation, insurance, and other such costs) would have cost about two dollars. On the other hand, if we'd gone in 1990, we would have found that the dollar had "fallen" sharply, so that it bought only five francs. Obviously a bottle of twenty-franc wine now costs us $4.

A falling dollar therefore raises the price of foreign goods, and a rising dollar lowers it. That is why, before we go abroad, we inquire what the exchange rate will be, and hope it will be "favorable." That is, favorable to us. But as economists we can never forget that foreign exchange must always be looked at from both sides of the ocean. A "good" rate of exchange for someone thinking about a trip to Germany will be bad to a German thinking of visiting the States.

These questions entered our consciousness with a vengeance in the mid 1990s, when the dollar made headlines as it fell from 112 to 78 yen in a matter of a few months. What was responsible for this "collapse" of the dollar (as it was often called in the newspapers)? As with all price changes, our first task is to look at the supply-and-demand situation.

THE MARKET FOR CURRENT TRANSACTIONS

Here we can best begin by mentally grouping all international currency transactions into two basic markets. If we bear those two markets in mind, we can easily understand why the dollar collapsed.

The first market is that in which the current transactions between firms, individuals, or governments are carried out. Here the demand for dollars comes from such groups as foreigners who want to import U.S. goods and services, and who must acquire dollars to purchase them; or from foreign tourists who need dollars to travel in the United States; or from foreign governments who must buy dollars to maintain embassies or purchase military equipment in the United States; or from firms abroad (U.S. or foreign) that want to send dividends to the United States or need to make interest payments in dollars. All these kinds of transactions require that holders of marks or francs or yen buy U.S. dollars on the market for foreign exchange, the international money market. By and large, you can do that at most large banks.

And, of course, there are similar groups of Americans who supply dollars to the foreign exchange market for exactly the opposite reasons. Here we find U.S. importers who want to bring in Japanese cameras and must offer dollars in order to acquire the yen to make their purchases; U.S. or foreign firms that are sending dividends or profits earned in the U.S. to a foreign branch or headquarters; Americans or foreign residents who sell dollars in order to buy lira or drachmas or kronor to visit or send money to friends or relatives abroad; or the U.S. government, which uses dollars to buy foreign currencies to pay diplomats' living expenses abroad.

Taken all together, these supplies and demands for dollars establish what we call our *balance on current account*. Until 1971, the United States regularly ran a small positive balance on this account, meaning that year in and year out we sold more goods and services to foreigners than we bought from them. Then, starting in the early 1970s we began to show small irregular *negative* balances on current account—occasionally buying more abroad than we were selling. Finally, in the early 1980s the irregular negative balances became regular and massive.

What happened to turn the current balance from black to red? The answer in part is the OPEC oil crisis, which resulted in a sharp rise in the number of dollars we had to supply to buy oil abroad. In 1972 our oil bill was $5 billion. In 1974 it was $27 billion. By 1980 it had grown to $83 billion—enough to cause a rise in the import of foreign fuel-efficient cars! In the late 1990s, we still suffer from a negative balance on oil of around $126 billion.

But oil shock was not the only reason for the falling U.S. merchandise balance. We have also experienced a long gradual decline in our competitive position vis-à-vis the other industrial nations of the West, a decline attributable in considerable part to laggard U.S. productivity. More of our machine tools and more of our consumer electronics came to be imported from abroad. As foreign countries cut the productivity and quality gap with United States products, Americans bought more of their products and their citizens bought fewer U.S. products.

When the quantity of any commodity supplied exceeds the quantity demanded, its price drops. When the supply of dollars needed for imports came to exceed the demand for dollars needed by foreigners to purchase U.S. exports, the dollar fell. It could not and did not defy the rules of economic gravity.

As a result of the high-valued dollar in the mid-1980s (something we will explain a little later), the U.S. current account deficit rose sharply, from $2.3 billion in 1980 to $116 billion in 1986. With Americans wanting to buy more foreign goods and services than foreigners wanting to buy U.S. goods and services, the value of the dollar started to fall that year and by 1989 had fallen 35 percent. With a lower-valued dollar making foreign products more expensive for Americans and U.S. products cheaper for foreigners our trade balance slowly and painfully improved. By 1990 the deficit was down to $31 billion, and in 1991 we actually balanced the current account, but in fluky ways: mostly because of payments we received from the rest of the world for fighting the Persian Gulf war and partly because we had a recession that cut our imports. When the payments for fighting the Persian Gulf war came to an end, and when the United States began to recover from the 1990–1991 recession more rapidly than the rest of the world, our current account deficits rose rapidly again—reaching $151 billion in 1995. With this enormous imbalance on current account the value of the dollar not surprisingly "collapsed" in the spring of 1996.

THE MARKET FOR CAPITAL TRANSACTIONS

But what falls can rise again. For current transactions are not the only purpose for which Americans buy foreign currencies or supply dollars. A second, quite separate market accommodates the need for dollars and other currencies to finance capital transactions. Included here are such transactions as building or buying plants and equipment abroad, or buying the stocks or bonds issued within another nation.

The first of these capital flows is called direct investment. It arises from the efforts of U.S. firms (mainly multinationals) to expand their ownership of plants and equipment abroad, and from the corresponding efforts of foreign companies to do the same thing here. The second part of the capital market is made up of U.S. or foreign individuals or firms who want to add to their overseas portfolio investments of stocks and bonds. Here we have Americans who buy stock in a Swedish firm or who buy German government bonds, as well as foreign investors who buy General Motors stock or U.S. Treasury bonds. Most important, foreign governments also buy and sell U.S. Treasury bonds. When they buy them they are effectively demanding dollars and supplying foreign currencies, and the value of the dollar rises and that of their own currencies falls. When they sell the exact opposite happens.

Adding direct and portfolio investment to the balance on current account can reverse the overall flow of foreign exchange. During the 1970s, U.S. corporations were expanding their overseas production facilities at record rates. This gave rise to a U.S. demand for foreign currencies on capital account that offset, to some extent, the net demand for U.S. dollars on current account. Then, in the early 1980s, the capital flow did a remarkable flip-flop. In part this was the result of a petering out of the U.S. expansion drive abroad, and the rise of a European and Japanese expansion drive into the United States. But in still greater degree it resulted from an unprecedented flow of foreign portfolio money into the United States. The anti-inflation tight-money policy initiated by the Federal Reserve in the early 1980s drove interest rates on three-month Treasury bills to over 14 percent! Not surprisingly, the economy slowed down and the inflation rate began to fall. The result was a kind of international suction machine that drew unprecedented quantities of foreign funds into U.S. Treasury and other bonds and investments to take advantage of the irresistible combination of high interest rates, falling inflation, and political security.

The result of this vast capital inflow was to prevent what would otherwise have been a self-correcting tendency in the foreign exchange markets. The poor showing of U.S. exports and the success of foreign imports should have resulted in a steady pressure *against* the dollar. This would have lowered the price of the dollar in marks and yen and other foreign currencies, thereby cheapening our exports for foreigners and making foreign goods more expensive for ourselves. After a time we would have expected our unfavorable balance on current account to even out, or at least to show a considerable improvement.

But the suction machine prevented that. Instead of falling, the dollar rose to such heights that our current account deficits became huge and our international economic position was no longer sustainable. There was a genuine fear that the United States was hopelessly priced out of its former markets, not just because of considerations of productivity, but because of the stratospheric dollar. By 1985 the dollar crisis had achieved such importance that a financial summit was convened among the leading Western nations to bring the dollar down. The big central banks of Europe and Japan agreed to sell dollars to drive down the value of the dollar on the international currency markets, even though this meant acting against the interests of their nations' exporters! They did so to prevent the ever-rising price of dollar-denominated exports, such as oil, from causing inflation in their domestic markets, and to prevent the dollar from crashing at some future point in time.

PROBLEMS OF HIGH AND LOW DOLLARS

Now let us consider the question of foreign exchange, not as Americans but as economists. Is there such a thing as a "right" price for the dollar, or for any other currency?

Like so many economic questions, this has a political answer. For the exchange value of a currency affects different individuals or groups or regions in different ways. Suppose the dollar is cheap. Obviously this is good for foreigners who want to buy a U.S. good or service, using their foreign money. It makes travel in the United States inexpensive for foreigners. It makes U.S. exports attractive. It makes U.S. stocks or physical plant tempting to foreign investors. All this rebounds to the benefit of U.S. exporters or hotel keepers or stockholders or owners who want to sell to foreigners.

On the other hand, a cheap dollar penalizes other groups. An American traveling abroad finds prices terribly high. A U.S. importer finds that foreign cameras, cars, sweaters are expensive—and so do his customers. U.S. firms thinking of investing abroad are deterred by the high price of foreign exchange. All this is bad for U.S. tourists, consumers, and investors.

Is there any reason for giving preference to those groups who benefit from the cheap dollar over other groups who benefit from expensive dollars? From the point of view of our national well-being, there is no particular reason to favor one over another. Is it better for a million consumers to buy cameras cheap, or for one hundred thousand steelworkers to have higher incomes? There is no cut-and-dried answer, only a contest of wills.

DEFENDING THE DOLLAR

We'll return to the problem of speculation on a global scale, but there is one last problem that we must address: whatever may happen to the stability of the world's exchange-rate system, can we not defend the dollar—that is, use national policy to cheapen it or make it more expensive, whichever seems best suited to our needs? Let us begin with the case where the dollar is falling, because that always seems worse than when it is rising. What can we do about a "weak" dollar?

One measure is simplicity itself: Prevent the flow of imports from rising. Anything that will turn the balance of merchandise payments in our favor will unquestionably alter the supply-demand situation and help the dollar go up.

Is this a sound policy? It will come as no surprise when we say that the answer is a political, not just an economic, judgment. To be sure, there are certain kinds of imports that we would like to diminish, not merely to defend the dollar, but to strengthen the nation. For instance, if we can substitute domestic energy (such as solar or coal) for imported oil, or if we can cut down on oil imports by conservation measures, the United States gains a much-needed measure of strategic independence as well as helping the dollar.

If, however, we cut down imports by blocking cheap shoes, textiles, or steel from abroad, we are simply protecting uncompetitive industries at home and penalizing U.S. households and businesses by depriving them of the right to buy shoes, textiles, or steel as cheaply as they otherwise might. We can sharpen the point by imagining that our tariff wall was sky-high. Then no goods would come into the United States. Would that be good for the United States?

On the other hand, imports cost jobs. Even if we compensate the workers in threatened industries, or help relocate them, or retrain them, some will not make the transition and will remain unemployed. There is a real human cost to competition—from abroad or home—that should not be lost to sight. We already have let something like a half million steel and auto and computer workers go down the drain to get cheaper steel, autos, and PCs from abroad. Is this a good exchange? Is the North American Free Trade Agreement with Mexico warranted in terms of the undoubted benefits it will yield to consumers or unwarranted because of the undoubted erosion it will inflict on U.S. job opportunities?

These are tough questions because they cannot be answered in a void. If we had strong systems of worker retraining, coupled with effective government assistance for industrial conversion, the NAFTA agreements would take on a much more attractive face than they do in their absence. (The same is true for the pace of cutting back our arms industry.) They are to be found in almost all other industrial countries, but are sadly lacking here. Once again, the success or failure of the private economy hinges more intimately than we tend to think on the support system provided by government.

Many economists would say that in the end, the benefits to the economy of having cheaper foreign goods, plus the benefits of moving our own resources and labor away from inefficient uses, outweigh the costs of unemployment. It would be interesting to see if they would come to the same conclusion if we were to import cheaper economists from abroad, asking our domestic practitioners to find another way of making a living. But even if we accept the conventional wisdom, we can see that there is a real conflict of interest involved in defending the dollar through restricting imports. At the nub of the matter is this political issue: Who is to gain? Who is to lose? Until that question is resolved we cannot really address ourselves to the economics of the question.

What about helping our exports? Many countries have tried to help *their* exports by giving subsidies of various kinds to their producers, so that they could sell their wares abroad cheaply. We have also subsidized some exports by underwriting our merchant marine, by arranging for special deals on U.S. arms sales to foreign nations, and by foreign-aid policies that have permitted us to sell large amounts of farm products abroad.

As with imports, it is not possible to give black-and-white answers about the wisdom of defending the dollar by export assistance. It may be in the national interest to sell $1 billion of arms on easy terms, or to export $1 billion of foodstuffs to the underdeveloped nations, but these policies should be judged on their own merits. The fact that they help defend the dollar is not, and should not be, a controlling consideration.

Policies to help exports or to hinder imports affect the balance of payments on current account. But there is also the market for foreign exchange for capital purposes. Can we defend or assist the dollar by intervening in that market?

We recall that there are two basic kinds of transactions in the capital market—direct investment, i.e., purchases of plant and equipment and other physical assets abroad; and portfolio investment, which buys stocks and bonds or simply parks money in bank accounts. One way of defending the dollar is simply to pass a law preventing the U.S. companies from acquiring foreign assets; and the opposite side of the coin is to push the dollar up by encouraging foreign companies to buy or build plants in the United States.

There is a great deal of immediate appeal to "keeping foreigners out"—an appeal that finds as much response among the Japanese who don't want U.S. computer companies in their own backyards as it does among Americans who don't want Japanese manufacturers in *their* backyards. In both cases the economist urges caution. Foreign investment by, say, Germany makes for employment in, for example, Tennessee—a consideration that is very important when we are considering whether or not to let foreigners in. And foreign investment by a Tennessee corporation may well lead to profits that come back to the United States—a consideration that must be taken into account in judging the effects of letting U.S. corporations build plants abroad.

Such reasons lie behind the general economic consensus that a fairly free flow of international investment is probably the best way to raise productivity and encourage economic growth, even though one nation may gain a little on another in the short run.

Note "fairly free." There are considerations of strategy and power at stake in the world of international economic dealings, not just profit and employment. Politics often asserts its priority over economics when considerations of investment are at stake. This is particularly the case when investment flows bring capital from the developed world to the underdeveloped world, a problem of great political and economic complexity about which it is difficult to make hard-and-fast generalizations. Hence, as with globalized trade, the position toward which we incline is one of overall support for the pushes and pulls generated by the market, accompanied by a willingness to intervene against the market, or at least to cushion its blows, when serious social and political considerations so dictate. That is far from a precise formula, but in an imperfect world it is the best we can come up with as a general guide to public policy.

THREE PROBLEMS, NOT ONE

How can we wrap up this complicated problem? Economist Robert Blecker has a useful way of disentangling its complexities.* He suggests that the United States faces three problems in the world of international trade and production, each calling for a different approach.

The first of these is unquestionably our competitive standing vis-à-vis our major industrial competitors such as Germany and Japan. Here the central problem is the lag in U.S. productivity, much aggravated in the case of Japan by its well-known reluctance to open its markets to imports. The latter problem, although extremely aggravating, has a relatively simple remedy: We can impose surcharges on Japanese imports unless Japan permits our goods to reach its consumers on the same terms that we allow Japanese goods access to ours.

The productivity problem is not so easily remedied. In the case of both Germany and Japan, their edge is not merely traceable to superior technological skills and strategies, but to a range of social policies that

*Robert Blecker, *Beyond the Twin Deficits* (Armonk, New York: M. E. Sharp, 1992).

greatly enhance the overall levels of efficiency in their nations. Japan and Germany both far outperform the United States when it comes to the physical and human investments necessary to raise productivity— investment in plant and equipment, the education of their youngsters, the training they accord their noncollege graduates—and in the active cooperation that marks the relations between industry and government generally. In addition, these countries have enjoyed a degree of labor-management cooperation visibly missing in our country—at least until recently, as we saw in Chapter Seventeen. It is also true that German or Japanese firms are more export-oriented than U.S. firms with their big home markets

That means that a balance in our trade with these competitors will have to be won, product by product, and year by year, through an effort aimed at a long-term elevation of the performance of the U.S. industrial economy as a whole that cannot be accomplished overnight. Nonetheless, the situation is far from black. In the 1990s, the United States regained its position as the world's largest producer of automobiles and semiconductors, something few thought possible in the 1980s. The United States is now running a trade surplus with the European Community, aside from Germany, and German superiority has been greatly hampered by the huge problems of merging its backward Eastern "half" with its modern Western "half," and by the high social charges needed to finance its extensive social welfare system. Meanwhile, a 1929-like crash has seriously wounded many Asian countries, requiring aid from the World Bank and Monetary Fund, as well as from the West, to prevent social as well as economic disaster. Although not so badly hurt, the Japanese economy is itself in the throes of reconstruction, so we have a breathing space in which to catch up with our competitiors.

The second main problem concerns the relation between the United States and the Newly Industrializing Countries (NICs). Our biggest bilateral trade deficit is no longer with Japan; it is with China! Here the difficulty lies at first glance entirely in the striking difference between their wage rates and ours. Workers' compensation in these countries is a quarter less than that of their U.S. counterparts. If these low wages just reflected lower productivity there would be no problem, because higher U.S. wages would be offset by higher U.S. productivity. Indeed, needing to import items such as capital equipment, developing countries should be, and often are, good markets for the products of high-wage countries.

But these low wages are only in part the consequence of a difference in productivity. They result, in considerable part, from repressive (anti-union) wage policies by the firms in NICs, buttressed by government policies designed to keep currency values artificially low. These low-paid workers are then combined with industrial equipment and techniques that are in many cases comparable, or nearly comparable, to our own. This can become a near-unbeatable combination.

Blecker suggests a different strategy for the United States. It is to encourage the NICs to allow their wages to rise to the levels justified by their productivity and to relax exchange policies that have depressed their currencies artificially. The NICs would undoubtedly retain a price advantage for many of their exported industrial goods, but it would not be so great that even the most efficient U.S. producers could not compete.

The last of the three problems overlaps to some degree with the second, insofar as it concerns the enormous problem of international indebtedness that weighs down some underdeveloped countries. In the 1980s the world's attention focused on Latin America; today it is focused on Africa. Many of these countries must use much, or all, of their hard-won export earnings to pay interest on their debts, rather than to buy the exports of U.S. producers. Latin America, for instance, was actually a net exporter of capital during the 1980s, as a consequence of having to pay principal and interest to its creditors.

What is needed, many economists agree, is forgiveness of a burden of indebtedness that now penalizes debtor and creditor alike. Such policies, along with internal reforms such as privatization and better systems of tax collection, got Latin America through its crises in the 1990s. Similar actions may permit at least some African economies to make their way into the 2000s.

All these proposals will be difficult to achieve, but as we have said before, difficult is not the same as impossible. They help us see that the international position of the United States is not beyond repair, although repair will not be easy. They also show us that much of the current difficulties stem from shortsighted U.S. policies of the past—failing to invest in projects to encourage productivity; ignoring the needs of our public household; carelessly lending money abroad, without a thought to the realistic chances of its repayment. To a large extent the United States is to blame for its own disadvantaged trade position today. That does not make unraveling its problems any easier, but it helps us recognize that we are responsible for at least a good portion of our present uncomfortable plight. The United States's problems weren't caused by foreigners playing the international game unfairly. This is a recognition that will be helpful if we are to attend to our international future as seriously as we should.

NINETEEN

The Unfinished Revolution

We have reached the end of our book, but certainly not the end of our purpose in writing it. *Economics Explained* was never intended to make economists of its readers. It has a much more down-to-earth purpose—to make economics understandable to them. We have tried to do so by taking away the language of economic analysis in order to consider the central question that technical language often obscures—a question we have all asked ourselves at one time or another as we listen to, or read about, the ups and downs of that mysterious thing called "the economy"—what is going on here?

We have sought to clarify that question in two ways. One of them is to demystify the economy by taking it apart. That is why we explain that the economy has a macro system that determines how much we produce and a micro system that determines who gets what share of it. In the same way, we try to explain what is going on by learning something about the role that government plays in the economy, including those much misunderstood debts and deficits it creates. Of course we explain how money comes into being. And then, after we have reduced the economy to life size, we try to make it still more real by describing the problems it creates, as well as those it solves—the subject matter of the chapters leading up to this one.

But there is another question about which we all think, on which our efforts at demystifying the economy around us shed little light. It is the question of our long-term future, of the prospects and possibilities for our economy over the long run—not the next few years, but the next few decades, or even more. To pose such a bold question makes us look at society from a vantage point that our down-to-earth approach cannot provide—a historical perspective that makes us aware of the extraordinary social dynamics that have brought us where we are, and in all likelihood will be the principal forces determining what we will be.

CAPITALIST REVOLUTIONS

The place to begin is with the realization that capitalism is a revolutionary system. We do not mean that it seeks to create political overthrows, like the French and Russian revolutions. On the contrary, capitalism has always been conservative, as are all established social and political orders. We do not mean conservative in the sense of opposing every change—indeed, capitalism, with its close association with democratic forms of government, has always been much more tolerant of political, social, and institutional change than have been older social orders, or for that matter, than were the socialisms that have tried to stamp out every deviation from a single officially formulated blueprint. Indeed, the Soviet Union can blame its downfall largely on that very unwillingness to adapt to changing realities, whereas capitalism is still very much with us.

Then what do we mean by the revolutionary character of capitalism? We mean that the essence of a capitalist order is to create change; and that this continuous generation of change has the effect of bringing about transformations in every aspect of life, social and political as well as economic. No such social system ever existed before. The Egyptian dynasties created marvels of architecture; the Greeks gave us unsurpassed art and literature; the Romans ruled virtually the whole world, as they knew it, for over six centuries, but none of them constantly revolutionized the daily lives, the social and political consciousness, or the history-making capacity of its peoples as has capitalism in a mere 250 years.

The revolutions of capitalism have been nonpolitical, in the sense that they arose in the world of doing and making, not ruling or philosophizing. Yet these changes have brought great changes in politics—consider the effects of radio and television on the relation between the electorate and its representatives and leaders, or the extraordinary social changes brought about by the conversion of a nation of farmers into one of factory or shop workers; or the enlargement of an individual's conception of his or her "place" in a society that gets around in wagons in the 1830s, in trains forty years later, in cars by the 1920s, that flies in the 1960s. Such changes are the rule, not the exception, under capitalism. They revolutionize the texture of life in a manner never known by the Egyptians, Greeks, or Romans—at least until the latter two began to experience similar transformations as their economies became capitalist around the eighteenth century.

So capitalism revolutionizes. It does not do so deliberately, however. Capitalism brings change because its single most important social class—those who possess or control "capital"—want to put it to use to make a profit. Profit-making—better, profit-searching—is the great engine of revolution for capitalism. That it changes the world in the course of its work is the consequence, not the central purpose of its powerful inner dynamics. Finally, not only is capitalism revolutionary, but in our own time we are experiencing one of its most far-reaching revolutions. That is the perspective we must gain to complete our understanding of what is going on here.

DYNAMICS OF CHANGE

Can we predict the outcome of the present revolution by looking back into the past? No. But we can see that it bears a family resemblance to past upheavals. Looking for these points of resemblance may forewarn of challenges ahead, and perhaps focus us on the areas in which counterpressures can be brought. They will also make it very clear that the present revolution, like those before it, will not be "turned off." It may come to a good end or a bad one, it may lead to a period of confusion or progress, but come to a stop it will not.

It may help to envisage the dynamics of capitalism if we look for a moment at the starting point of most transformations—a newly invented or developed product or process that brings about new economic opportunities that later bring social and political repercussions. We can easily call to mind a half dozen such seeds of revolutionary change: the newly created division of labor that Adam Smith recognized as an unprecedentedly powerful means of increasing output and thereby enhancing profitability—accompanied, let us recall, by his concern that this same marvelous source of productivity would dull the intelligence and curiosity of those who were forced to perform its relentless repetitions. Then there was the steam engine that made possible the economical extraction of coal by providing the cheap energy to pump water out of the mines and bring coal to the surface, from which sprang the Industrial Revolution. Thereafter came the revolution of electricity which, productive effects aside, literally lit up the world and created a new period of social time called "night life." Next came the internal combustion engine, giving us the automobile that changed everything; and not too long after, the extraordinary adventure of flight, once thought of as the prerogative of angels and adventurers, to become in the years following World War II the underpinning of the world's largest new industry, tourism.

And in our day? The revolution was born in the bulky computer but achieved its extraordinary penetrative power with the minuscule silicon chip. From the chip came the explosion—no less dramatic word will do—of communication, and from the explosion came an extension of overview and management that extended from a desk located almost anywhere to sites of production also located almost anywhere. Globalization would not have been possible without the chip, just as the extraordinarily rapid unification of the continental United States would have been impossible without the railroad, or the creation of the modern city without steam and electricity.

All these technologically based revolutions have their initial effects on the organization of business, the manner in which capitalism amasses capital. Capital, we recall, is not "wealth." By wealth we mean the physical embodiment of power and prestige, like the great palaces of antiquity. By capital we mean the use of wealth to increase itself— palaces used as real estate. New factories or buildings are thus not wealth, in the original meaning of the term, but links in a chain of transactions in which wealth takes on the form of a commodity—anything intended for sale, hopefully at a profit over its cost, the money to be reinvested in more of the same or different commodities that will again be sold for a (hoped for) profit—ad infinitum.

In a capitalist world many things can be used in this endless spiral of expansion—mere coal is as good as fine silks. Invention is thus not necessary for capital accumulation, but it gives it a special impetus by providing new products and processes to energize the process: new commodities displace older ones, or as who knows what product, still in the lab, will one day give us the invention that will displace the chip, as the chip has displaced the dry-cell battery.

FROM PRODUCTION TO SPECULATION

We are obviously in the throes of a revolutionary change in which the effects of economic stimulus have become spread across the globe, not concentrated in a single nation or group of nations. As we know, its directing agency is the multinational corporation—the institutional creation of the computer.

Here the original effect was the rapid increase of investment among the nations of the developed world, up four-fold during the 1980s. Toyota, to take a well-known example, remained a Japanese firm, but its car became, for all intents and purposes, American. There is virtually no major corporation, U.S. or European, that does not now make its goods in other countries, or "outsource" to other countries parts of the products it sells in its home country.

More significant is the relation between the developed and the underdeveloped worlds. In the past, the revolutionizing impetus of technological change gave rise to expansions that for a long time remained mainly within their countries of origin. It took decades for the effects of the industrial or electrical or automotive or air revolutions to reach the undeveloped nations. But in the current revolution, computerization leads to the outflow of capital wherever high-tech management can be combined easily with low-wage labor. Hence the outsourcing, or direct investment, now involves areas of the underdeveloped world that were previously of only minor importance in the capitalist world. Vietnam, Thailand, Sri Lanka, the Philippines, Indonesia—along with China—are places that participate, although still only to a small degree, in the current capitalist revolution. Taiwan, South Korea, India, and parts of South America are enmeshed in it. This is undoubtedly good for their economies, and for the profits of the multinational corporations, but it is not so good for the work forces of Europe or America who find their real wages stagnant or falling, and their employment imperiled, as their employers downsize and automate to take fullest advantage of what the new technology offers at home.

Now comes a phase that we have not looked into previously but can trace back through virtually all capitalist history. The first rush of all revolutions arises in its new industry and spreads to other industries through chains of economic linkage down to the corner grocery store. But within a few years this initial phase of generalized expansion begins to give way to another area of dominant interest. This is the movement, then the rush, of money capital into the markets for securities. Without exception, the revolutions of capitalism begin in the factory and move to the stock exchanges.

A new problem now intrudes on the revolutionary impetus. The financial boom that follows the boom in production is much more volatile than its more slowly expanding source. Financial markets can rise and fall with astonishing abruptness because they are driven largely by expectations of future prices, not by the conquest of actual markets. Hence, in place of the steady upward climb of expanding sales, which gradually gives way to a plateau and then to slow decline, financial booms can race heavenward and fall back to earth with dramatic suddenness, as we all know from the devastating conclusions of the boom of the 1920s that ended in the devastating crash of '29.

No one knows if there will be such a conclusion to our present financial boom, but there have been some alerts. We have just read about a narrow escape in Asia, not yet safe and sound. But look back at our own recent history. In 1987, the U.S. stock market fell almost overnight from a record high of 2700 on the Dow Jones industrial average to a low of 1500. European markets quickly followed. Thereafter, the Dow Jones began to rise again, until by 1997 it topped 7000. This was tantamount to a judgment that the financial worth of the companies traded on the exchange had more than quadrupled in less then ten years! Then came October 27, 1997, when the Dow Jones fell by 554 points, the greatest single drop in its history. Moreover, this precipitous drop was matched or exceeded in virtually every capitalist nation in the world. It was probably the greatest single one-day financial debacle in world history.

Does this supercrash augur a deep depression along the lines of that ushered in by the stock market collapse of 1929? That seems extremely unlikely, if only because governments around the world have learned not to repeat the fearful errors of that earlier day. Photographs of the '30 banking crash show long lines of men and women waiting in vain in front of banks to draw out their savings accounts. In those days governments sincerely thought it would be "inflationary" to guarantee the liquidity of the banking system!

Then is the crash a warning? Yes. Of what? Of the persisting social dynamics of the cycles of real growth and speculative boom that have always characterized capitalism; of the fact that capitalism moves through history by lurching ahead and stumbling back. And of one more thing, to which we now turn.

THE FOREIGN EXCHANGE MARKET

Into this two-century-old sequence of technological change followed by financial speculation has come a new, highly disquieting development. It is connected, as we may have guessed, with that great sea of foreign exchange that has followed from the technology that brought us globalization. But to understand it, we must begin by clarifying the difference between a fixed and a flexible (or "floating") exchange rate. A world of fixed exchange rates is not one in which some superpower establishes the prices at which the world's currencies will exchange—no country possesses such transnational legal powers. It is, rather, a world in which one currency generally is recognized as the linchpin of the international world, usually because it is the currency of its political hegemon. Thus the British pound in the late nineteenth century and the U.S. dollar in the years following World War II were the key currencies in the fixed exchange regimes of those times.

This did not mean that England could legislate the number of dollars that a pound would be worth in the same way that it could declare, in those vanished days of the gold standard, the amount of gold that the pound must contain. Rather, the meaning of "fixed" exchange rates meant that the hegemonic nation and a few of its main trading partners agreed that they would use all their legitimate powers to "defend" the price at which the linchpin currency exchanged with the partners' currencies—say five dollars to the pound, give or take a few percentage points when special circumstances caused a rush of buying or selling orders on one or another of the currencies.

Such declarations in themselves were stabilizing because few users of foreign exchange, including speculators, would buy or sell currencies lightly at prices higher or lower than these limits, knowing that the hegemon and its "partners" would then utilize their large reserves of the currency in question to bring the exchange rate back to "normal." As we have seen, the dollar played this role very successfully for nearly twenty-five years after World War II, when changes in the world economy led finally to its abandonment.

By contrast, a world of flexible, or floating, exchange rates is one in which there is no such hegemonic power, and as a consequence, no agreements to keep—or at least to try to keep—the relations among currencies within well-defined bounds. Instead, the value of pounds and dollars and francs and yen are established by the workings of a vast, interconnected market for currencies in which buyers or sellers anywhere can put in orders to buy or sell currencies of other countries at any price they wish, without fear that they are bound to lose shirts. These orders may be placed to finance actual transactions or simply to speculate, just as on the stock market shares can be bought or sold to add to, or reduce, one's assets, or because the trader is "sure" he or she knows which way the stock is going, and wants to get there before it happens.

In the case of the exchange markets in the 1980s, after the United States stopped being the monetary hegemon, speculation soon took over. Currency values roared up and down: the dollar rose by 64 percent from 1980 to 1985 and then plunged back to where it had been in the first place; the yen fluctuated wildly; the lira "collapsed" (more than once), even the "dependable" German mark was often under attack. This took many economists and central bankers by surprise.

They had thought that the collective judgment of knowledgeable dealers in foreign currencies would bring about a smoother, less volatile market than one in which bureaucratic governments hesitated to adjust fixed rates, despite warning signs of changing economic conditions. In fact, foreign exchange markets came to be dominated by speculators with very short-time horizons who jumped on and magnified short-run ups and downs into major booms and busts. In a replay of the speculative drama that capitalism had enacted many times before, the volume of foreign exchange transactions grew to immense size, soon overpowering the ability of central banks to impose some degree of stability and order. In *One World, Ready or Not*, economic journalist William Greider has described vividly the erosion of the power of these banks. In 1983, he points out, the central banks of the United States, Germany, Japan, Britain, and Switzerland held $139 billion in foreign exchange reserves to be used to stabilize an average daily turnover of $39 billion in foreign exchange. The bankers therefore had a three-to-one advantage over the speculators. By 1992, the balance of strength was reversed: The major central banks had $278 billion in reserves against $623 billion in daily trading activity. The market traders now had an advantage of two to one. They had their way. Within a few years the volume of foreign exchange dealings rose to the $1.3 trillion-a-day wave of dealings that we have noted.*

Alas, it did not turn out to be the easy road to riches that had captured the minds of speculators. In 1994, for example, Procter and Gamble lost $137 million; Metallgesellschaft of Germany lost $1 billion; Glaxo of Britain $160 million; Orange County, California, $1.7 billion; Bank Megara, the Malaysian central bank, $4 billion. Even George Soros, one of the most daring and successful international speculators, who had made a multibillion-dollar fortune for himself, lost $600 billion virtually overnight when he was caught wrong-footed one week in early 1994. As to who lost how much in the crash of '97, we do not yet know.

As a result we now hear voices calling for a return to fixed rates, including a warning from George Soros that a continuation along the present lines opens the way for global disintegration.†

POSSIBILITIES

There is little doubt that the replacement of fixed by flexible foreign exchange markets has changed what was once a source of considerable global stability into a new hurricane breeding ground. Hence the first question is: can we do something about it?

No one will be surprised that our answer is Yes and No. Nobelist James Tobin, for example, has proposed a tax to be imposed on speculative purchases of foreign exchange. Such a tax certainly would cut down the number of speculative transactions, and might thereby dampen or avert speculative swings. But then again, it might not. For one thing, an antispeculation tax would be of little use were it imposed by only one country. Foreign exchange trading would simply shift to less tax-minded markets. Even if all major nations agreed to impose the tax, rogue markets would almost certainly be available for those who sought them. This is certainly not an argument against trying to secure a transnational tax on speculative exchange transactions—it is merely a reminder of the difficulty of doing so in a world that is hardly composed of like-minded nations.

Here is a second difficulty. Suppose speculators decided to buy cur-

---

*William Greider, *One World, Ready or Not* (New York: Simon & Schuster, 1997), p. 247.
†Greider, p. 257.

rency X, even though it was falling, because they believed the fall would end quickly. Their purchases would, of course, help make that expectation come true. But if there were a tax to be paid, win or lose, the speculators might decide the game was not worth the candle. In that case the tax would have worsened, not eased, the pressure against the currency.

What is to be done in the face of such difficulties? It is all too likely that nothing will be done, in which case we would sooner or later suffer a serious foreign exchange debacle. Such a crash could easily bring multibillion-dollar losses for companies all over the world, and would inflict painful losses on many small holders of mutual funds who probably had no idea their money was also partly in the exchange market.

BACK TO REVOLUTIONARY CAPITALISM

The nineties have been a period of stunning growth for America. Then why do we end our book on a note of warning? It is certainly not to warn our readers of an impending crash. It is rather to bring us back to the theme of this chapter.

That theme is not that our system is headed for disaster of one kind or another. The uncontrolled foreign exchange market is certainly an area in which capitalism might do something quite self-destructive, but *self-destruction* is not the full meaning of "revolutionary" capitalism. Rather, the term means two things: first, that a capitalist system contains expansive energies that can bring unexpected, unwanted, and sometimes seriously threatening consequences for the continued smooth working of the society; and second, that the system also contains the capability to meet these threatening changes with institutional changes that can greatly lessen, or even remove, those negative effects. Unlike any other social order—especially that of socialism in its Soviet form—capitalism thus contains a self-corrective potential, all the more needed in view of its constant tendency to create difficulties for itself.

History is certainly full of examples of the first of these tendencies. The Industrial Revolution, with its newly created restive proletariat, was one such; the development of mass production, with its trustification of business, was another; the Great Depression that descended upon us in the 1930s was yet one more; and in our day globalization—the most disruptive and trouble-making aspect of economic life—also has been brought about by capitalism's own dynamism. Ahead lies one more instance of a "revolutionary" challenge in the slowly emerging challenge of global warming with its far-reaching ecological ramifications.

How were these self-generated challenges met? The Industrial Revolution called forth the first government regulation of basic labor conditions. Trustification was the source of the first antitrust laws. The Great Depression was tamed by the New Deal. What will be the responses to globalization and ecological deterioration? The remedy will not emerge from the intervention of benign aliens from outer space. It will have to develop spontaneously within the dominant socioeconomic framework of the twenty-first century, which is to say, within capitalism.

A LAST WORD

All this has a moral for our tale and provides a proper ending to it. In much of the West, and especially in our own country, government is today much criticized and denounced. There is often good reason for that antipathy: governments can be—and perhaps always are—bureaucratic, slow-moving, inefficient, and irritating. They are not repositories of unsullied virtue, exemplary foresight, stirring vision.

What they are, however, is the only means by which a body of people can provide itself with that which it cannot obtain elsewhere: foreign policy and defense, law and order, the provision of public capital, and—crucial for our purpose—a counterforce against the unwanted effects that emerge from the private sector. That counterforce may not always be effective—there are plenty of unsolved problems in capitalism—but it is the only such capacity that exists.

In a word, no complex society can exist without government. That is why the public sector is as much a part of a capitalist order as is the private sector, which could not long exist if government were somehow to disappear. We should not forget, moreover, that the functions of government under capitalism are not only to provide defense and public capital and law and justice, but also to act as a kind of gyroscope or a steering mechanism when the nation needs a balancing counterweight or a hand on the steering wheel. There will assuredly be such situations in the years ahead, as globalization and then global warming become ever more insistent problems that require powerful guiding and containing forces.

Here, as so often, economic analysis goes just so far. In the end, large-scale changes require not just an adaptive revolutionary capitalism, but the elusive contribution of things that lie outside that framework, such as the collective temper of peoples and the wisdom or folly of their leaders. Hence it seems proper to end *Economics Explained* with the admonition that we must come to understand our subject, not to achieve a Good Society, but to prepare ourselves for the really difficult problems that we will still face after economics is understood.

Index